STARWASHED

The Chad Reynolds Story

Chad Reynolds

To Ginny

DEDICATION

I dedicate this book to my parents, Richard and Pam Reynolds, who stuck by me through the worst of times. No matter what happened to me on my journey through life, you were always there for me. I can only imagine what it must have felt like to watch your child go off the deep end of life. Especially when the child wasn't raised like that. I will forever be grateful for all you have done for me. God bless you.

CONTENTS

ACKNOWLEDGMENTS

I would like to acknowledge all the friends and family that stuck by me through my darkest days. Thanks to my ex-wife, Veronica, who tried her best to love and support me, even though I didn't deserve it. Thanks to the AA fellowship for showing me how to live a comfortable, alcohol-free life. And finally a big hats-off to Bob Proctor and the Proctor- Gallagher Institute for teaching me the paradigms of positive thinking.

CHAPTER 1: INTO THE WORLD

Some authors have a tortured, tearjerker of a childhood from which to launch a compelling autobiography. But not me. I was just a vanilla White kid born in rural America, on Christmas day. Hey, wait – *that* was special. I came into the world in Corona – a small town in Riverside County, California. Well, it *used* to be a small town. It's grown to be quite the size in recent years. Most people from outside of the state ask me:

"Is that near Los Angeles?"

"Sorta, but no," is the short answer.

See, there's this issue with the 91 Freeway that makes it a day trip. Too many cars – not enough freeway.

I had blonde hair, blue eyes, ten fingers and toes. My parents named me Chad Allan Brown the night I was born. A dashing name to set me on a stalwart path. My mother brought me home from the hospital on Christmas Eve. The nurse wrapped me up in a Christmas stocking. I heard that she rubbed my little cheek and cooed.

"You ruined mommy's Christmas dinner."

It had to be a sign because I would be the ruin of many a holiday dinner in the decades to come.

My mother had my older sister, Karyn, three years before me. I was the second of her three kids. My biological father worked in construction at the time. He wasn't around much. Their relationship didn't last to my first birthday.

We moved a lot, going from apartment to apartment. We all lived with my grandmother for a while. My mother always had odd jobs to make ends meet. She just concentrated on us two kids, at first. I hear we were a handful. She started dating off and on. In the process she met the man she was to marry. Richard Reynolds become my Dad, making *me* Chad Reynolds. A stalwart name indeed. It would take most of my life to live up to it.

Richard went to college at night to become a civil engineer. During the day he went to work to support us two kids. Now, as I look back, *that* made him a hero. In 1974, my Dad and Mom were married. They bought their first house in Orange, California. It was there, that they had my little sister, Kim. But they soon realized, after only a year, that the house was too small. They sold it and bought a bigger one, not too far away, in Santa Ana CA.

As a child my hair was a bit longer than most kids. I was a super blonde 'toe head.' My mother always dressed me in overalls. The neighborhood adults referred to me as Dennis the Menace. The neighborhood families got a kick out of me as I ran around the neighborhood. For those too young to know, Dennis the Menace was a TV show about a mischievous kid who was always in trouble.

I wasn't old enough to start school, but my sister was. She walked to school every day. You can't do that these days. I stayed home playing with my mother and my new little sister. But she couldn't do much but eat, sleep and cry. I miss those times of innocence and unlimited imagination. Most adults have had their imaginations beat out of them, by a system that wants us to conform, so that we can be controlled in mass.

In 1975 my parents had found a new house back in Corona. That's the house I was pretty much raised in, since I was five years old. That house was safe, secure, and full of love. It was a respite from the outside world. Funny, how we think the world should treat us with love and support. Well guess what? The universe was created to keep us safe and warm. It will too. If we let it.

Too often, through negative thinking, we impede the

universe's desire for us to prosper. We remain in contentious situations that we could easily leave. We remain there because we fear the unknown. Even when our physical bodies are trapped in intolerable situations, our minds are free to escape. And in the words of that old 'funk' band Parliament/Funkadelic,

"Free your mind and your ass will follow."

The house was on a majestic hill, along with 14 other beautiful homes; all custom built just 500 feet from a clubhouse. Our backyard was adjacent to the first fairway of a well-manicured golf course. The backyard was completely fenced in, to stop sliced golf shots from hitting us. Our house had been one of the model homes – four bedrooms on a quarter acre lot. It seemed so much bigger when I was a child. It seems small now, at less than 2,000 square feet. Life is like that, when we learn to see beyond our current circumstance.

I started kindergarten that year, at Coronita elementary school, about a mile from our house. Me and my sister walked there every day. Our street dead-ended at the country club parking lot. But there was a small pathway between two houses. We'd walk through it on the way to school. *Those* neighbors called me Dennis the Menace. My sister tried to keep me on the straight-and-narrow.

"Don't step on the flowers, Chad."

"Why not," I answered. "They're already dead."

"They're dead because you step on them every day. Step over em' like me."

"Maybe. When I'm taller."

I attended school there, from kindergarten through the second grade. Until my parents sent all three of us to a Christian school in Riverside, California. This school was unlike the public school systems. They didn't require a uniform, but if you did something wrong, the teacher would swat you on the butt with a big wooden paddle. I never got a swat, but I heard many other kids cry as they got theirs. I completed third grade without trampling a single garden. And I learned to conform. Conform or be punished.

My older sister was always getting into trouble at school. She got the heat taken off me, as my parents shifted their focus to her.

"Did you step on some flowers or something?" I asked with

all sincerity.

"Shut up, Chad," she snapped back.

My younger sister was oblivious to what was happening. She was only a toddler. But I was glad for the 'air cover' that my big sister put over my own mischief.

After a year and a half in a Christian school my parents put us all back in public schools. The Christian schools had gotten way too expensive for all three of us to attend. I was halfway through the fourth grade when I returned to Coronita elementary.

It was then that my Dad decided to adopt me and my older sister. My mother ran an ad in the Press Enterprise stating that an adoption was pending. If my biological father wanted to contest it, now was the time to step up. He never did. I was eight years old when my older sister and I had our last names changed to Reynolds.

Richard was no longer my *step-dad* – he was the man that stepped up. I didn't understand the significance then. To me, my dad had always been Richard Reynolds. Today I realize what a big deal that was and how hard it must have been for another man embrace the woman he loved *and* her two children.

When I was nine, my Dad had me baptized at the church we attended regularly. I didn't understand the significance of the event. But I understood that it was an act of love. Dad was a good Christian. He said he took us to church to meet Jesus. And maybe I did meet Him. Maybe He kept me alive for me to give you this testimony.

As I grew, I established many neighborhood friendships. My best friend was Jason. We roamed the golf course together, in the open green fairways, and rode our bikes and skateboards. We did most of our hanging out in Jason's neighborhood because my house was on a hill – not really a kid friendly place to ride bikes and skateboards. Most of our friends lived by Jason anyway.

Jason lived in a cul-de-sac, off a street named Monterey Peninsula. There were four cul-de-sacs off that street. Our friends lived on three of the four. Not far from Jason's house, there was a dry creek bed, just below the Cleveland National forest. It ran all the way to the Santa River. Whenever it rained hard the creek surged to life. That place became my second home. Where rules gave way to imagination.

Our imaginations are a special gift from God. They allow us to see what has yet to exist. The imagination is the seat of all great accomplishments. And, if we allow it to flourish, we will live a full and diverse life. We will accomplish what others dare to even dream.

We spent all of our free time on the creek bed, building forts, riding bikes, and hunting for small rodents. One evening, just before dusk, I saw something moving.

"Jason, there's a possum behind that bush. Pump that bee-bee-gun ten times."

"I don't think it's a possum, Chad."

"It is. And it's coming this way."

"That's not a possum. It's too big."

"Well what else could it be?"

"It could be a wolf or something. And it's getting dark. Let's go home."

"Gimme' that gun, you wuss."

Jason was glad to oblige. As Jason backed away, I pumped that gun until it wouldn't pump anymore. I took aim at the thing, just before Jason yelled.

"That's not a possum. It's a SKUUUNNK!"

Too late – for me anyway. I took milk baths for a week. And for that whole week my parents called me Dennis the Menace.

Along-side the creek bed there were two tar pits. They were fenced off by the county, so that imaginative kids like me (idiots) couldn't get in. But we were too young to know (or care) why. But they did have a strong odor, and when we threw something over the fence, it would land on the tar and sink. We always thought that was so cool but we never hopped the fence. This time I heeded Jason's warning.

"If you drown in that tar, they're gonna arrest *me* for murder."

We loved getting up at the crack of dawn on weekend mornings and putting on our camouflage clothes to hunt mice. Possums were nearly the size of skunks, so we didn't go after them anymore. Jason saw them as wild pets or something anyway. That smell of damp sage brush, trees and bushes, in the early morning air lingers to this very day.

We always wanted to stay at Jason's house because his parents were not as strict as mine. And he lived close to the wash. Jason's father was a very early riser. He made sure we were up and out the door by first light. Hmmm –maybe he didn't like me. Whenever it rained we couldn't play in the wash because our parents said it was too dangerous. So, we would head to my house on the golf course. There, we would go rafting and playing in the swift waters rushing through the golf course. Danger was my middle name.

CHAPTER 2: GOLF BALLS AND ALCOHOL

By ten years old I'd already started on an entrepreneurial streak. Rain and flood waters often filled the duck ponds on the golf course behind my house. My next-door neighbor, Steve, was a few years older than me. He was being looked after by his grandparents. We came up with a great idea. We'd wade in the ponds and comb the entire course, to collect lost balls and sell them back to the golfers at a discount.

Every Thursday and Friday night we collected balls, and washed them clean in my yard. On Saturday and Sunday morning I would arrange the balls in two piles. In one pile, there would be almost new balls – we sold those, two for a dollar. The piles with the not-so-new balls, sold three for a dollar.

Not long after we started selling golf balls, Steve's grandmother started making coffee and cookies for us to sell to the golfers. We wrapped the oversized chocolate chip cookies in plastic wrap. We served the coffee from hand-pumped thermos jugs.

We used what little money we made from our first sales to buy coffee, foam cups, cream and sugar. The entrepreneurial spirit was alive and well within me. We repeated our early morning routine and were at the fifth hole tee box by dawn. Golfers are a dedicated bunch. And so were we.

As I started junior high, my older sister was starting high school, and my younger sister was in elementary school. I can still remember those cold mornings waiting at the bus stop with all the other kids. The bus ride to school was not nearly as exciting as the one on the way home because school was over and it was play time. After we did our chores, of course. While watching cartoons, of course.

For a while me and my older sister traveled on the same bus. She made sure we got the chores done. She'd be the one to get in trouble if we didn't. I liked my big sister, so I did my part. Both my parents didn't get home till after five. My mom picked up my baby sister, who was in the afterschool care program. She saw to it that we got our homework done.

My father was working for the city of Corona, as a civil engineer, and mother sold real estate. Most weekends she was at work. So Dad kept me close to him – to keep me focused, he said. After selling golf balls and coffee on the course, Dad had me help him in the yard. We'd sit together and eat lunch, then go back outside to work.

My sisters were there with Dad too. But he was trying to show me a good work ethic. Being the only boy, he had me help him with the yard work. I couldn't wait for him to say I free was to go, so could ride my bike. I'd go find my friends, thinking it odd that they didn't have weekend chores like I did. But it taught me a lot about growing up and becoming responsible.

I was always thinking of ways to make a buck or two. I bought black and white spray paint, stencils and masking tape. I loaded it all in a small bucket and started going door-to-door painting house addresses on curbs. That endeavor netted me a little money here and there.

I also had my mom take me to the local thrift store to buy cinnamon oil and tooth picks. Then I made cinnamon flavored tooth picks. I packaged them in tin foil and sold them at school. One day I was caught by a teacher and sent to the principal's office. I had to stop, to please my principal and parents. But that didn't stop me from moving on to something else that would make me a buck or two.

When I was younger, my family didn't partake in many outdoor activities like camping, boating, dirt biking etc. But a lot of my friends grew up with parents that *did*. Steve had the coolest parents. Every year they went camping on Lake Mead, in Las Vegas. One year he asked his parents if I, and another friend, could come along.

"Can Chad and Mike come with us. Please?"

"Ok, but they need their parents' permission."

The next day Steve asked me if I wanted to go?

"You should come with us, Chad," Steve beamed. "It's the coolest. But you gotta get your parents' permission. Get a note or something."

"I don't know Steve. My parents are pretty strict."

But I went home with high hopes. And that night I asked my parents about the trip.

"Can I go, please. Steve's parents said I could go."

"Have we met them before, honey?" my dad asked my mom.

"I don't think we have. You're only 12 years old, Chad. Maybe next year."

"You could at least call them, Mom. Come on, I never get to go anyplace cool."

My dad gave me his 'don't push it' look, so I shut up about it.

That night after dinner my mother phoned Steve's parents to get more information on the trip. I was doing my best to read my her facial expressions to determine whether it was going to be a 'yes' or a 'no.' About midway through the conversation I had a feeling it was going to be a 'yes.' As she hung up the phone smiling she looked at me and said:

"It sounds like it should be fine, but you have to ask your dad."

I looked at my father. *Well?* He just smiled. I was going to get to go camping. I was so looking forward to it that I didn't pay much attention in school that next week.

A few days before our trip, Steve's mother took us to the store to buy provisions. We loaded up the shopping cart with food and snacks. Then we came to the liquor aisle. That's when

Steve and Mike started loading cases of beer into the cart. I was shocked.

"What are you doing?"

"Getting beer for our trip," Steve answered.

"You can just do that? Your mom doesn't care?"

"She's paying for it," Steve answered with a wink. "You never had a beer before?"

I had never even held can of beer before. But I lied.

"Between cokes and other drinks, I might have a beer or two a day."

Mike and Steve looked at each other and laughed, while they loaded more cases of beer into the cart.

I didn't mention the shopping trip to my parents that night. If I had talked to them about it, they would have surely changed their minds. Looking back, I wish I had. This camping trip would be the start of a downward spiral that would later cripple, and almost kill me. I didn't know that I was born with the genes of an alcoholic mother.

That weekend we set out for Las Vegas. It was a long four-hour drive in a cramped motor home. When we finally arrived, I was very excited. The smell of the outdoors reminded me of the old creek bed. I felt freedom in the air.

We met two other families at the campsite. They camped with us, but had their own motor homes. The camp was about 500 feet from the water, and there was a 10 foot ledge that separated the upper campsite from the lower one, down by lake.

That first night, all of us kids made a camp fire down by the lake. We intended to spend the night down there in sleeping bags. The adults had their own camp fire up by the motor homes. One of the other families had a young teenaged daughter named Avon. She was slender, cute and shy. I eyed her like a hawk. Her parents called her to come up and go to bed.

But later that night, Avon snuck out of her parents motor home, and came back down on the water to hang out with us. We all sat around the fire laughing and drinking beer. Avon stayed quite most of the time, in fear her parents would hear her, and scold her for sneaking out. I wanted to get this Avon girl to notice me because I was so attracted to her. I figured if I could impress her she might take a liking to me. Every time one of us threw an empty beer can into the pile by the fire everyone would cheer.

Right then, I knew what I was going to do to impress her. I started drinking only a quarter of my beer and then I secretly poured the rest out behind my chair. Then I'd toss it into the pile. My friends cheered.
"Way to go Chad! You're the man!"

Over an hour of drinking quarter cans, I had consumed probably four or five actual beers. All of the sudden, I didn't care about Avon anymore. This weird, new, exhilarating feeling rushed through my body. It was like I'd found what I'd always been looking for. And I *was* 'the man.' I got up out of my chair and hollered something stupid and ran and jumped into the lake with my clothes on.

When I came out of the water everyone was laughing. I later learned that they were laughing *at* me, not *with* me. The commotion woke up the adults. My friends laid me down on my sleeping bag and told me to be quite. But I didn't care. I didn't want to be quiet.

Then I heard adult voices.
"Avon, are you down there?"
And again, my friends begged me to be quite.

As I looked up the small ledge, all I saw was two *fuzzy* sets of couples. They seemed to be spinning round and round.
"Avon, you come up here now!" one of the fuzzy men demanded.

Steve's parents were the second couple I saw looking down the ledge. I could tell they weren't happy about what they were witnessing. When Avon went up to the motor home the excitement died down.

By now I my head was spinning like a fallen leaf in the wind. And I was nauseous from all the beer. I got sloppy drunk the very first time I drank alcohol. I spent the next 30 minutes throwing up, all around my sleeping bag, which was already soaking wet from that jumping in lake stunt. All the while I was cursing at my friends and telling them I would never touch alcohol again as long as a live. I finally passed out.

The next morning the adults weren't saying much to each other. I personally felt like a train had hit me. Both of my friends kept telling me that one cold beer would make me feel better. After an hour of suffering, I took their advice. I found myself wading in the lake with a cold Corona beer in hand. It did make me feel 100 percent better. That was the first sign that I was going to have an alcohol problem as I got older.

CHAPTER 3: HIGHSCHOOL DAZE

This is where the fun begins, and fortunately for me I was one of the blessed ones. I really admired my older sister, Karyn. Not only did I admire her because she was my sister, but now she was old enough to do all the cool things that adults did. She had a car and a job. She was self-sufficient with positive cash flow.

One of Karyn's first jobs was at a local video store. I remember this particular night she'd been working late. I was at home, as usual, when she came home with a gift for the family. It wasn't just any gift. It was the coolest gadget around. The owner of the video store gave Karyn a brand-new VCR. In 1985, a VCR was cutting-edge technology. I remember feeling very special. Not a *bragging* kind of special – but grateful.

After that night, my sister brought home movies of all different genres. We enjoyed them *together* on our brand-new VCR. And I began to realize the *real* value of money. You could have nice things, and you could pay for them all by yourself. But for the lifestyles I saw in some of those movies, you had to have a lot of money.

I developed a curiosity about how the financial world worked. I wondered what it would be like to make some *real* money – enough money to buy whatever you wanted. But how could I pull it off. As much as I loved those special family moments. I couldn't wait to grow-up and leave the house – so I could be independent and do whatever I wanted.

Shortly after that I took on my first paper route. This was right up my alley. I liked working early, and being done by the time other people got out of bed. And once a month I went door to door for my collections. I got talk to adults. Which I loved, because it made me feel like I was more mature than my friends. And *that* made me feel important.

My plan back then was to get through junior high and move on to high school, where I could get my driver's license, and start working to make bigger money. It seemed like forever, but I finally made it to high school.

In the 10th grade I took a driver's education course and got my learners permit. I needed transportation if I wanted independence. I could take advantage of greater opportunities if I had a car. *And* – girls liked guys with cars. I saved money from my jobs. Those jobs were actually businesses. A had a golf ball and snack business, a paper route, a curb sign painting business, and a cinnamon toothpick business (until they made me stop).

I finally saved enough to buy my first set of wheels – a motor powered scooter. My friend Jason's dad got me a deal at the Yamaha store. It only went 45 mph, but it was perfect for getting to school and work. And besides that, I could ride it with just a learner's permit. If I drove a car I'd have to have an adult with me.

Another opportunity presented itself immediately. Just after school every day, I would drive my scooter to Warren's RV dealership. I washed and cleaned up used motor homes that were for sale. Warren also had me wash and wax his Corvette once a week. Oh man, how I looked up to him. I tried to be the best employee he had. But the job didn't last long because I wanted more hours than he could offer. Warren was setting limits on my worth. It was better to be my own boss.

But the certainty of a paycheck still had me sold on the idea of selling my time to make *someone else* wealthy. So I got another job right around the corner, at Naugles fast food restaurant.

You could see the big Naugles billboard from my backyard – it was that close. We'd go there after we sold golf balls and spend money from our sales to eat. In a sense, I was trading my time for food.

I rode my scooter to work after school, and at odd hours like 3:25 am, depending on the schedule. I worked, or *got* worked, 30 hours a week. They even gave me a uniform: brown polyester pants, a Naugles shirt, penny loafer shoes, and a paper Naugles hat. I traded my time for a pittance. *And* let them use my body for a walking billboard.

There was a manager named Reba, who'd worked there for a number of years. She was a bitter woman in her sixties, with grey hair put up in a bun under her paper hat. She smoked cigarettes. And she took long breaks with *other* people that smoked cigarettes. Believe or not, I started smoking cigarettes to fit in, and get longer breaks. So, yeah – I was trading my health to work at a job where everyone's personal satisfaction came from break time.

I seemed to have a lot in common with my manager. Which meant that I was acting like a bitter old chain smoker who lived for longer smoke breaks. I guess I got tired of having smokers cough, and thankfully smoking didn't really stick with me. My older sister put in a good word for me at her previous job, at the Mad Greek restaurant. She worked there before she started at the video store.

So I went in and filled out my application. They hired me for 10 cents more an hour than I got at Naugles. After I left Naugles, I swore I would never touch a cigarette again. But my new job was a few miles further away. Now I was trading my raise for gas, to get to the job. Which was probably a fair trade, as long as I was riding a scooter.

I was the fry boy. I fried French fries, zucchini, onion rings, etc. I actually loved that job because I had responsibly. My manager, Mr. lee, came up to me as I was working.
"You're doing a fine job, Chad. I'm going to give you a 10 cents an hour raise."
I couldn't wait to go home and tell my parents the news. Isn't it amazing that we get excited when someone tells us

we're worth a dime more.

My father had been in the grocery business at one time. He was convinced that the best job for a young man like me was a box boy. From that position you had a chance to move up the ladder to cashier. So he kept prodded me to get a job at a local grocery store. But every time I went to see the store manager, he'd say:
"Sorry. We're not hiring now."

One day, as I was pulling away on my scooter, I saw a friend who *was* a box boy there. He was out collecting carts in the parking lot. He gave me a tip.
"If you want a job here, wear a tie next time."

The following week I did just that. I was hired on the spot as a box boy. I was one proud young man, and I couldn't wait to tell my dad the news. He was proud of me too. They started me off at $3.75 an hour. I hustled, and ran through the store, always doing the best I could for my cashiers and coworkers. I learned two lifelong lessons from that experience. Dress appropriate for the position. And that I am more valuable if I'm helping others earn money.

I took up tennis that year. And I took to it like a fish to water. I loved to play, so I kept my racket and a can of balls bungee-corded to the rear rack on my scooter. I kept a skateboard back there too. I was always prepared to do whatever my friends wanted to do, *after* I was off work. I felt like the *king* of the street I hung out on. I had a candy apple red scooter, and I was the oldest of our friends. I had what I thought was the dream job for a kid my age. All I needed now was a driver's license.

I took the test as soon as my age allowed. I was ready for my first car. My dad got a loan from *his* credit union and we found my first car – a grey 1966 Mustang for $50 a month. My scooter just sat in the garage taking up space. I sold it for a couple hundred dollars. Life should've been great. My friends really envied me. But my ego wasn't satisfied.

I let (or led) the crowd I hung with to believe I was already sexually actively. In truth I was a virgin. Meanwhile I was dating this girl from school named Susan. Well actually, I was in her friend zone.

I was at her house one night when her parents were out of town. And, Oh my God, we had sex. The next day I was hanging out with my friends. I wanted to brag about my conquest in the worst way. But I couldn't say anything because they hadn't known I was a virgin. There has to be a lesson in there somewhere. Ok here's one: honesty is the best policy.

A new supermarket was about to open, and push the market I worked at out of business. I got a job there before they even opened. I gave notice at my current job. They weren't too happy, but they understood. But I quit too soon. The new job was still a month out. I had a car payment to make, *and* my insurance was due.

At school, my grades were average at best. My mind was on making money, not on schoolwork or scholarships. My friend, Robert, told me about this vocational high school just down the street from Corona high. It was a school for kids like me, who just wanted to work, and had no desires for higher education. They got out at 11:40 am every day.

I begged my parents to let me go there.
"Come on guys. I'm not going to college. I just wanna work."
They had conditions of course.
"Only if you agree to return to Corona High in time for graduation. You *know* it's a family tradition."

I got accepted at the vocational school. Now It was time to find another job. I applied at a local car wash. The pay wasn't great, but tips took up the slack. And I still had my golf ball business on weekends.

I got out of school early, which left a couple hours open before work. One day I was driving along, laughing with my friend, Mike. I wasn't paying attention. I accidently ran a red light and got broadsided by another car. The crash sent my Mustang sliding sideways across the intersection.

I was looking around to see if the car that hit me had stopped. When I turned back I saw a semi-rig heading right for the driver's side where I sat in wide-eyed shock. The semi had the right of way but he couldn't have stopped in time if he tried. I watched as those oncoming headlights got bigger...then Bam!

I didn't even hear the crash. I only remember waking up in an ambulance with my head and body in restraints. *And*...the paramedics trying to revive Mike. That was one of the worst feelings I've ever had in my life. My friend lay dying, and it was my fault. He came too, screaming in pain as they tried to start an IV. I felt helpless and I was to blame! *What if he dies? What will I say to his parent? Or to mine?*

I was alert and sobbing. I couldn't even wipe my tears because my hands were strapped down. Because I was more alert than Mike, they kept yelling at me.
    "What kind of drugs are you on?"
    "Nothing," I wept. "I swear...nothing."

It was a long ride to the hospital. And longer still before I found out if Mike was going to survive. But he pulled through. Thank God, Mike pulled through. It was well into the night when I was finally released. But to my surprise, Mike had been released to his parents, a few hours earlier. I thought for sure my parents were going to be mad, but all they said was:
    "We're glad you're both ok. Now let's get you home."

Mike was back in school the next day but I wasn't so lucky. I couldn't return to school for a few weeks. The doctor said that I'd fractured my pelvis and that there was nothing that could be done to fix it.
    "You need lots of rest," he told me. "Pelvic fractures take longer to heal than arms and legs."

The car wash gave me time off. I didn't go to school because I couldn't walk. A few of my friends came by after school to wish me well. After a few weeks on the couch, I was back in commission. My Mustang was not. It was a total loss. And I'd sold my scooter. *Now what*?

My grandmother had given up her driver's license, so she let me use her 1968 Cutlass Supreme. My parents had rules for *this* car though. And one of them was that I couldn't take it out of town. In other words, I could only drive in the little city of Corona.

I started dating this girl, Mariah, from school. She smoked so I started having an occasional cigarette. One Friday night we went on a double date in my grandmother's Cutlass. We all sat close, in that big couch of a front seat, as we drove down a dark street late at night. I looked down and tried to grab Mariah's hand with my right hand. I had a lit cigarette in my left. And Bam! *Again with the Bam*! It hadn't been more than three months since my last accident.

I'd hit a parked motor home. The hood of the car flew open on impact. And there I was, yelling at my friend to get out and close it, so I could flee the scene. But his door was dented in the crash and wouldn't open. It was two o'clock in the morning. I couldn't see spit. The hood was stuck open, and the headlights were smashed. I drove, leaning out of the window, looking for a well-lit road.

We finally turned onto a street that had street lights. We all got out of the car and looked at the damage. And then they clowned me.
"Wow, Chad. Where'd you get your license; Kmart?"
"Whew! Dude – maybe you should let somebody else drive."
"Weren't you just in a car wreck – like last month or something?"
I just shook my head and thought, *my parents are gonna kill me.*

I went home and lied to my parents.
"A drunk driver hit me and drove off."
I never did go to the owners of that motor home. Not even to apologize, let alone to pay for damages. Guilt finally set in and I confessed to my parents what I'd done. They sold Grandma's car, as is. They left it up to me to go and make amends. I never did. No punishment was ever received. But the scars of guilt cut into my soul.

My parents' grace only made me feel worse. They helped me buy a used Toyota, crew-cab pickup, in mint condition. It was the mid 80's when mini-trucks were all the rage. In no time, I had the chassis lowered, and slapped on low profile tires. I customized the interior too.

But my friend, Robert's, parents got him a show-truck that was already decked out. So I put a hard-shell cover on my truck bed and installed a high power stereo system. I thought that material things would heal whatever ailed me: a cracked pelvis, or even a guilty conscience.

I left the car wash and went to work at the new gas station that opened just down the street from my house. One night, after drinking with friends, I stopped off at the gas station where I worked to get a pack of cigarettes. We all went inside. I left the truck running with the stereo booming. As we came back out, I wondered why my truck was rolling. *Maybe I forgot to put it in park*. Then some scumbag stuck his head out of *my* window and gloated as he raced off in my truck. And it was gone – right before my eyes.

Guilt, you see, must be punished. Some even called it Karma. But if we internalize unresolved guilt, we will actually punish ourselves. I fixed up that truck with money I should have used to pay for my trespasses. Since nobody punished me, I was bound by the laws of universal justice, to punish myself. But I didn't know about universal laws at that time.

I cried. Yep, I cried and called my dad to come get us. And as he pulled up and got out of the car he asked:
"Which one of you are sober enough to tell me what happened?"

I still didn't realize that something was terribly wrong with my character. I had an attitude of entitlement. Not that I thought anybody owed me anything. But I put me, and my stuff, ahead of other people's basic wellbeing. How else could you explain the amount property damage and wasted money that I'd racked up in less than a year.

All I could see was the time, and money, that *I* put into *my* truck. And since it was something *I* treasured, *I* shouldn't have had *my* property disrespected that way. *I, I, I, me, me, my.* But I had disrespected the owners of all the property that *I* had damaged.

CHAPTER 4: MY FIRST ARREST

I was well into high school. I felt like a grownup. And I drank often – outside of the house. Just months after my truck was stolen, I was relaxing at home with my parents one evening – just watching TV. The doorbell rang and I jumped up to get it. It was my friend Robert. Robert worked at the local tire and rim store. That night after work, he stopped by to show me what he'd stolen from work that day. I put on my coat and told my parents I was going outside to talk to Robert.

"I'll just be a minute."

When we got clear of my house he pulled a long, slim tool, from under his coat.

"What the hell is that thing?" I asked.

"It's a slim-jim."

"And?"

"You know, like when you lock your keys in your car. This thing unlocks the door from the outside."

I thought about it for a moment.

"Prove it. Use it on your truck."

He locked the door on his Nissan truck and then unlocked it from the outside – fast and easy. Then he told me the reason he'd come over.

"How about we go steal a car stereo somewhere?"

"I don't want to get in any trouble."

"Come on man," he pressed. "Look at how easy this is."

He didn't have to press very hard.
"Ok, I'm in let's do it."

I told my parents I was going out for a while. We drove about 10 miles to a Park-n-Ride parking lot. People parked their cars there and then carpooled to work. We got out and started roaming the lot, looking in car windows, for a high-end car stereo. It wasn't long before Robert yelled out.
"I found one – over here!"
"Here I come," I said, rubbing my hands together like I was some kind of big time *cat* burglar.

It was a late model Mazda truck. I acted as lookout while Robert started to unlock the truck with his Slim-Jim.
"Hurry up dude. It's freezing out here," I urged through chattering teeth.
"I'm going as fast as I can. You just make sure nobody creeps up on us."

After 10 minutes I was starting to get nervous.
"What's the hold up?"
"It's a tough one."

Another car pulled into the lot. I turned to Robert.
"Screw this! Let's go. A car just pulled in!"

Robert stopped what he was doing and we started walking back towards his truck. But for some strange reason, the car that pulled in didn't parked. It just stopped in the middle of the entrance with its lights on, and engine running.

Robert got spooked. We were about five feet from his truck when he tried to toss the Slim-Jim into the back of his pickup. But it bounced off the tailgate and landed on the ground.

By then we were both frantic. Robert picked up the slim-jim and tossed it in the truck. That car just sat there. We couldn't see the driver. Here's the best stupid idea we could come up with; we popped the hood on Roberts truck and pretended we had car trouble. It was obvious we weren't having car trouble.

After another five minutes of us just starring at Roberts motor, and the car just sitting there, we decided to get the heck out of there. We slammed down the hood, jumped in the truck and took off.

As we pulled out of the Park-n-Ride, the other car pulled out right behind us. I yelled at Robert.

"Oh crap!"

Robert gunned it.

I saw a police car coming from the opposite direction – headed straight for *us*. A hand came out of the window of the car behind us, and pointed towards us. I put my hands over my face.

"Were doomed!"

Robert couldn't see what I saw.

"What's happening?"

I didn't take time to explain.

"Drive faster! Drive faster!"

Robert was driving a lowered, stick-shift, mini truck, so we hit 65 mph in just a few seconds. We smoked that cop car – until we came up to a railroad crossing.

"Watch out for the..." I never got the last word out.

All hell broke loose when we bottomed out on the tracks. We bounced around, banging our heads against the roof like popcorn in a pan. We had no choice but to pull over. And by this time there were more police cars than I could count. A sea of red and blue flashing lights converged on us, to the sound of wailing sirens. I jumped out of truck to make a run for it. I didn't run a single step.

"Get down on the ground. Now!"

I've never had so many guns pointed at me. I held my breath while they patted Robert down. They didn't know if he had a gun on him or not. For that matter, neither did I. After a weapons frisk that came up empty they holstered their weapons.

The first officer walked to the truck and shined his flashlight around in the bed. He didn't see anything suspicious. *I might get to go home*, I thought. I was just a passenger. But the second officer looked more thoroughly and pulled out the long black slim jim.

"What do we have here?"

"I have no idea where that came from," Robert lied.

Then the woman from the other car walked up and identified us.

"Yep, that's them."

And that was that.

It turned out she was a locksmith. She initially thought one of us was a locksmith too. When she realized we were breaking into someone else's car, she radioed the police, and waited on the scene for them to arrive.

We sat handcuffed on the curb for what seemed like an eternity.

"Ok, bro," Robert whispered. "No matter what happens we keep quiet."

"Ok cool," I told him. "I ain't telling-em nothing."

About an hour went by, with tow trucks arriving, and lots of police chatter. Eventually one of the officers walked over to us.

"Robert, please stand up."

They placed him under arrest. I knew that I was next.

We were both arrested and taken into custody. We were questioned at the Corona police station. I remembered me and Robert's agreement. But I was already shaking. But by the grace of God I heard Roberts voice coming through the vent from the other room.

"Just tell the truth."

I did. And we were charged with attempted burglary. Because we were minors, they allowed our parents to pick us up. But that was in the 80's. Now-a-days it most likely wouldn't have gone down like that. I wish I could tell you that, *that* was the only time I was arrested. But, sad to say, there'd be plenty more arrests in the years to come. My parents were devastated – but not surprised.

When we went to court, I was tried as a minor and received a sentence of five weekends in juvenile hall. I remember my first weekend. My mother sat beside me in the intake waiting room. A sheriff came out and made an announcement.

"All weekenders, please come with me."

My mother leaned over and kissed my forehead.

"I love you. See you on Sunday."

I almost died of embarrassment because the other guys saw

my mother's touching farewell. My head hung low as we walked into the changing room. One of the other boys looked me up and down.

"You're gonna get it up the ass," he smirked.

Meaning I was going to get raped. I didn't. But I was still scared beyond belief. I thought for sure my life was over. My five weekends went by quick. It was just a slap on the wrist. I learned no lesson.

When all was said and done, my parents blamed the vocation school for my errant ways. They said it was because the school gave me too much freedom. In the 12th grade, I went back to Corona high, just like I'd promised. Maybe I could fool my parents, *and* myself, for another season.

But when the first-quarter report card came out, I was in danger of failing every single class. Of course, I blamed it on the schoolwork being completely different than what I was taught at the vocational school. To make matters worse, I had just turned 18. I was considered an adult, and I could write my own excuses. When I said was sick, they didn't call my parents. I was setting myself up for a fall. I was sick *a lot*.

I tried to improve my grades when graduation got close. But it was too little, too late. The registrar wrote my parents a letter saying that there was no way I was going to graduate from Corona High, that semester. *I* really didn't care. But my parents were highly upset with me.

I went back to the vocational school and begged them for help. They set up a plan for me to get extra credit by writing book reports and pushing lunch carts. So that's what I did for the remainder of the 12th grade. And I ended up graduating, on time, from Buena Vista Vocational High School.

CHAPTER 5: GOOF BALL

I lost my job at the gas station for goofing off. I managed to get hired at the Corona car wash – in between goofing off. It wasn't my dream job, but it got my parents off my back, and helped me pay what little bills I had. After about six months a man, Collin, came through the car wash. It must have been a special day on my part because he said he was impressed with my work ethic and drive. Go figure.

Collin gave me his number and said to call him. He was a drywall journeyman in need of an apprentice. The housing tract he was working on was just above my parents' house, up in the hills. At the time the minimum wage was four dollars an hour. He said I would make six. I was in heaven, or so I thought. I started the following week. He taught me how to hang drywall. Over the next year, we became good friends.

Because I had a good job, my parents stuck their neck out for me *again*. They co-signed for a late model, red Toyota 4x4, so I could get back and forth to job sites.

Some kind of friend Collin turned out to be. One night he split town and took my weekly pay with him. I was astonished to say the least. Two days later I called the company we worked for, hoping they would keep me on. I had a new truck payment to cover. But they were angry at *me*. They didn't even want to talk to me.

I put my feelers out and found another apprentice job hanging drywall, taping, repairing and patching. I couldn't see it at the time, but I was stuck in a rut. Job after job and boss after boss, deciding my financial fate.

There was this restaurant that operated during the day, but at night and on the weekends, it operated as a night club. One night my friends (Mike and Jason) and I were there diggin' the music and dancing. The night was winding down and the last call for alcohol was announced.

I wasn't ready for the night to end, so me and my two friends drove to the gas station. We made it just in time to buy a 12 pack of beer, before they stopped selling it for the night. We took our beer and drove my 4x4 onto the golf course by my house.

I did 'donuts' on the wet grass, with my stereo turned up as loud as it would go. Then we raced around the wet golf course screaming and tearing up the grass. At 3:30 am we decided to split before somebody called the police.

I was traveling at good sliding-speed when all of the sudden my rear tire caught a sprinkler valve. The truck flipped, and tumbled, finally coming to rest on its side. I started yelling.
  "Get out! Get out!"

We were all drunk off our keisters. They opened the door and tried to climb out. Since the truck was on its side, the door slammed shut, throwing them back down on me. And I lay pinned, between them and the wet grass, outside my open window.

We eventually made it out. We tried to lift the truck back on all fours, but it kept sliding on the wet grass. Then we heard a neighbor yelling from his backyard.
  "What are you kids doing back there?"

None of us could think of an answer, so we took off running, in different directions. I ran to my house. I got home in a panic. I woke up my dad, and told him what happened. But I told the 911 operator something else.

"Help! My truck was just stolen!"

She transferred the call to the police, but it took him two hours to get there. In the meantime, I was eating chocolates and drinking lots of water, in an attempt to sober up before he arrived. An officer finally showed up at the front door.

"Your truck was found, less than a mile away, abandoned on the golf course."

Oh really, I thought, but I didn't dare say it.

"Yeah, I just reported it stolen."

I knew that *he* knew I was lying. But he had no proof.

What a long night that was. I thought the police were gonna come back and arrest me. So at 6 am, I returned to the scene of the crime. I watched a tow truck load up my truck, as the sun began to rise.

My two friends waited until the coast was clear, before they called me, to get the scoop on what happened. I got my truck back from the autobody shop, two weeks later. My insurance paid for the repairs. Wow, that was close! Another lesson not learned.

Then I met a girl who stole my heart. Her name was Gina. She was a 15-years-old, slim Hispanic girl with long brown hair. She was still in high school and had very strict parents. I fell so hard I bounced. I had butterflies in my stomach. I don't think I was even eating.

We talked on the phone for hours. Her bedroom window was at the front of her house. And I'd stand outside it, whispering sweet nothings in her ear. When her father got home from his swing-shift gig, I'd run and hide in the bushes until he went inside.

At the same time, I was staying out late and drinking. I moved on to smoking and selling marijuana. My stock sure dropped fast. I became an embarrassing liability to Gina. She broke it off with me. She said she wanted to be with her high school friends instead of being tied down.

I felt like the world had ended. I couldn't sleep, or eat, or even work. I was constantly calling her, crying and telling her how much I needed her. They call that stalking now days.

I eventually got my own apartment. Gina came over a few times, but we never got back together. I was too self-centered. I was 19 years old with a 4x4 and an apartment. I worked hard, and at the end of the day I deserved to get wasted. What more could I have asked for? More money, that's what. So I rented a room to my old buddy, Steve.

We mostly sat on the couch smoking cigarettes and pot. I drank beer after beer while we smoked. Steve seemed to have a hard time keeping a job. I guess my misery loved company. I sold pot to cover the shortfall.

It was a normal summer day. Meaning we were sitting on the couch getting wasted. We were startled by a fist pounding on the front door. I confidently jumped open and flung open the door with a friendly hello.
"GET ON THE GROUND!"
"What? Holy..."
"GET ON THE GROUND NOW!!"

Talk about a black hole. That's all I saw, with that cop's gun pointed in my face. So yeah, I got on the ground. Five more officers swarmed on top of us. As I laid there on my stomach, I had flashbacks of my first run in with the law. I came really close to peeing my pants. And maybe I did – just a little.

Steve looked over at me with the innocence of Gilligan (from Gilligan's Island). I would have used Gilligan's last name but he didn't have one. Or maybe Gilligan *was* his last name. In any case, I finally 'fessed' up.
"He didn't do anything. It was all me."

Steve couldn't sell weed if he tried. He would've just smoked it all up. They uncuffed him. Then they bagged up all the weed. And all paraphernalia. And all money I had in the bedroom closet. Busted, would be an understatement. This time I was thrown into a jail cell and slapped with a substantial bail.

As I sat in that cell, waiting to be transferred to the county jail, I looked out the small window to the outside world. I couldn't see myself getting out of this one. My parents were done with me. I couldn't even tell the bail bondsman who to call. I was shaking my head, thinking *kiss your ass goodbye,*

Chad – when the cell door opened.

"You made bail," the guard snapped. "You're free to go."

I actually looked around, but there was no one else in the cell.

I found out later that one of my customers put his house up for my bond. Now *that guy* was my friend. As soon as I got out I had called Gina – *not* the guy that bailed me out. I tried to explain why I hadn't kept in touch. She didn't care. She was just pissed. *I was the one that got arrested. What did she have to be mad about?* Then I called the guy that bailed me out.

"Thanks, man. You didn't have to do that."

"Yeah, I know," he said. "You have so much potential. Why are you wasting your life?"

I didn't have a real answer.

"I'll try and do better."

"Just make sure you show up for court. And remember you owe me one."

The tougher call was the one I made to my parents. I told them what I'd done and that I would try to do better.

"Sure, Chad."

Click.

I found out later, that *another* customer ratted me out, to get his 'possession of marijuana' charges dismissed. Without selling drugs, I couldn't afford my apartment. And what about my truck note? The nerve of that guy, putting his own interests before mine.

I got a good lawyer – another favor for my sister, Karyn. The only thing on my record was attempted burglary, from the car stereo incident. And I really put on a show. I was a sweet boy that made one bad decision. The judge gave me unsupervised probation and a small fine. My lawyer couldn't believe I got off so easy. Neither could I. Everybody loved my sister, Karyn. Maybe she knew the judge too.

I was still doing construction – only living back at my parents' house. My 4x4 needed new tires – and expensive tires at that. But I had no extra money. Robert's dad owned a big-0 tire store. Robert said he could get me a good deal on tires at the warehouse supply center. So I went to my Grandma and asked her if I could borrow the money. I was still playing the role of the sweet misguided boy (Dennis the Menace), so of course she said yes.

The following week I went with Robert's dad to go pick up my tires. Grandma's sweet boy had been up all night doing crystal meth. I was down in the dumps (withdrawal symptoms). Robert senior must have noticed.

"How are things going, Chad?"

For some reason I just let it all out. A cathartic purge came from deep in my soul.

"I can't keep living like this. Everything I touch turns out wrong. I can't keep a job. I live with my parents, and they barely speak to me. They're ashamed of me. Heck I'm even ashamed of myself. If it were anybody else, I'd be calling them a loser."

Maybe I am a loser. He must've read my mind, because he was shaking his head from side-to-side.

He tried to offer solutions to my problems. And then he said:

"You know what. I've got this mobile car wash trailer. I tried to start a business with it, but it didn't pan out."

I'm thinking, *what's that got to do with me?*

"Really?"

"Why don't you give it a try?"

Ok, *then* I got it.

"REALLY?"

"Try it out for a few weeks, and if it works out, we can discuss a payment plan."

"Ok. I'll give it shot. What've I got to lose; right?."

"Right."

The trailer was a custom made, two axel affair. It looked like a rocket ship molded around a three hundred gallon pressure wash tank. And emblazoned on each side were the words "Star Wash 2000."

I already had my 4x4 to pull it, and now I had new tires. So that next day I drove to his house, hitched it up, and towed it away. I called in sick to my construction job. I spent the day knocking on doors trying to drum up business. I could pressure wash anything: cars, mobile homes, driveways, whatever. And I would beat anybody else's price.

After four days of towing the trailer around and knocking on doors, I quit my construction job to start my own mobile wash company. I didn't even have any customers yet.

"You're crazy," came from the lips of many.

I went back to Robert senior and we struck a deal. I was going to buy it for $3,000. He agreed to let me pay him $200 a month, until it was paid off. The next day I bought office supplies. I turned the cluttered desk, in my bedroom, into a well-organized work desk. Even though there wasn't anything to do, I believed that there soon *would* be.

I was encouraged by the few washes I did that first week. I went (with my dad) to the supply store. I bought wash-n-wax car soap and tire dressing. I was extremely grateful, and I envisioned big business. I continued going door-to-door asking my neighbors if they needed anything washed.

It wasn't long before I exceeded my pay as a drywall construction worker. I'd found my niche. But the trailer was old and the pressure washer was in constant need of repair.

I found a guy, Carl, who owned a pressure washer repair shop. He gave me all the free advice he could. But I was fighting a losing battle – like a housefly stuck in a window sill. I was gonna have to up my game, or go out of business. Carl came up with an idea.

"Why don't I custom build you a brand-new pressure wash trailer?"

"How much?" I asked with bated breath.

"Five thousand. But I'll finance for you, for...say...250 a month?"

It was an offer I couldn't refuse.

"Deal."

Robert senior graciously took back his old trailer.

Six months later, one of Karyn's many friend's rented me a room, with access to the garage. He happened to live right across the street from my old friend Jason. He worked a lot, so I had the large four bedroom house pretty much to myself.

I worked every day to build my business. I was self-employed. Nobody could limit my hours or my pay. I set my own schedule and prices, so it was up to me to decide my worth. Between jobs I drank beer. And since I was the boss, I could drink beer whenever I wanted.

I was on a mission – a mission of self-improvement. I proudly enrolled in college. I took two night courses: Business and Spanish. But my academic endeavor was short lived. After a full day of work – and beer, I decided I'd rather spend my nights resting up for the next workday. I few more beers helped me relax. College didn't. So I withdrew from my classes. Maybe I'd go back when life wasn't so hectic.

My landlord found his true love, and they wanted their privacy.
"So, Chad. Me and Mary think it's time for you to move out. It's not personal, so no hard feelings – Ok?"

I was dumb-founded. The nerve of this guy to put his sex-life ahead of a fine, upstanding tenant like me. I ended up finding a small warehouse for my business, and a house about 45 minutes away to rent with an option to buy. One more time, I went begging to my parents.
"I only need you to co-sign. Just for the house, not the warehouse. You don't have to pay for anything."
After a few days they agreed. Or, maybe I just wore em down.

After closing both deals, I became a commuter. I lived so far away that nobody wanted to make the drive to come see me. I lived in a neighborhood of older folks, so making friends was difficult. I used those excuses to rationalize my ever increasing thirst for beer.

After racking up back to back dui's, during the commutes to and from work, my driver's license was suspended. Then the housing market collapsed. The house I had agreed to buy for $109,000 was now worth only $85,000. I couldn't afford to get caught drinking again with a suspended license. And I knew it would be only a matter of time before I did.

I told myself I was sick of driving so far everyday anyway. So I just bailed on the whole contract, and left my parents 'holding the bag.' I rented an apartment close to my shop, while my parents paid for the breach of contract.

CHAPTER 6: BARSTOOLS

I'd grown to look like, what most people would describe, as a surfer dude. I had blonde hair, blue eyes, and I kept a killer tan because I worked outside. So a lot of people referred to me as 'that surfer looking guy.' I only say that, to tell you that I didn't have to *fish* for women. They usually just jumped in the boat. While other guys were focused on getting laid, I was focused on getting drunk.

There was this guy, Scott, who owned a boat repair business. A dirt field stretched between his shop and mine. He had a lot of business and needed a detailer to shine up those power boats after he fixed the engines.

We became good friends. Scott was short and stocky guy who loved to drink beer just like as much as I did. We drank together pretty regularly. By then, I was smoking more than a pack of cigarettes a day. His wife, Kathy, was a slender blonde who worked as a secretary. She drank as much as we did.

We liked to get drunk, while driving to NASCAR events, in his motor home. And we drank at their house, which was about 25 miles from his shop. They got prequalified to buy a larger house, just up the street from his shop. They asked if I would rent a room from them to help cover the new house payment. I didn't even have to think it over.
"Sure, I would love that."

Things couldn't have been better. I got out the apartment I'd rented, after I could no longer hide my drinking from my parents. My rent was way lower. *And*, I was gonna live with two people that drank like me.

I met Scott's best friend, Dave, while I was living there. Dave owned a large aluminum factory. He did very well for himself. He had a gorgeous wife and a newborn daughter. His house and cars were a testament to his success. To say I was envious of his lifestyle would be an understatement.

He drove around all day with his brother, Mike, drinking beer from a cooler. Some days he'd meet Scott and I for lunch at different bars around town. But most of the time lunch lasted the rest of the day. We rarely made it back to work afterwards. On occasions we went golfing in the morning and then to the bar right after the round. And it was always a sure bet that we wouldn't make it to work *at all* on those days.

We took frequent trips to the Colorado river with three or four couples that had motor homes and boats. Dave's, of course, was always the biggest and newest.

One Sunday we went to the local bar to watch the NASCAR race. But it got rained out for the day. The next day as I sat in my office, I pictured myself living Dave's carefree lifestyle. *I own this place and I have employees out working. I can leave whenever I want.*

I convinced myself that it would be just dandy if I jumped in my truck and went back to that bar. Oddly (to me) there were no customers inside. The place even seemed too clean to be a bar. At first I felt very strange, but the bartender already knew me.
    "Good morning, Chad. What will it be?"

I never drank beer at a bar – I just didn't see the point. I always ordered vodka and cranberry juice. But it was breakfast time, and I didn't want to seem like a common drunk. So I thought it more appropriate to order:
    "Vodka and orange juice."
    Just then my cell phone rang.

"Star wash can I help you?"

"Hey, Chad. It's Scott. Can I bring a boat over for you to detail?"

"I'm not there," I whispered. "I'm at the bar – the one from yesterday."

"What the hell you doing there this early?"

"I'm gonna watch em' restart the race."

"You're crazy," he laughed. "I'll call you later."

Well that felt like the pot calling the kettle black. Another drunk was insinuating that I drank too much. But maybe – just maybe, Scott wasn't an alcoholic. And maybe I *was*. After two drinks it didn't matter. The morning drinks always made me feel splendid. But now I was drinking in the morning – alone.

I started spending more and more time in the bars. I lost all taste for beer and started drinking vodka, exclusively. I showed up at Scott's house pretty much blasted, every night. Scott and his wife called me in the living room one night.

"Hey guys, what's up?"

"Chad, don't take this personally..."

Uh oh, here it comes.

"but we're about to start a family. And we're thinking maybe you should find someplace else to live."

But they weren't really asking. *Oh well another one bites the dust.*

I befriended a man in the bar named Mark, who lived in a nearby apartment complex. He was looking for a roommate. I had to choose associates that were at least as bad as me. He was a drunk too. So I moved in.

He worked in construction for his brother. We both had early start times. But I could wake up to a morning drink because I was the boss. He couldn't because he wasn't. We had that apartment for six months, and then we moved to another apartment for about a year.

My love life was crazy. I was with a different girl every time he saw me. I wasn't the kind to settle down – my drinking would never permit it. Mark hooked up with this girl named Stephanie. She was known as the town drunk. She got super belligerent whenever she drank. And she drank every day. They fought like cats and dogs every night. I'd finally met my match.

Their alcoholic behavior was worse than mine. I couldn't take it (seeing my own bad behavior in others). I moved out.

My favorite watering hole was 'The Depot.' Over the years I developed a lot of friends there. One particular man was named Eddie. He was short Hispanic man who'd retired early in life. He was single, and rented a house not far from the bar. If there was anyone in that bar who could out drink me – it was Eddie. He got to the bar early, drank all day, then went home and passed out. The man rarely ate food. He more-or-less lived to drink.

He was talking to me early one evening. He said he heard about my living situation. He offered me a room to rent. I jumped at the opportunity. He was a quiet drunk who passed out at night. And he didn't care how much I drank. I was all moved in, in a week.

You could set your clock by Eddie's routine. He showed up at a bar called 'The Lounge' at 6am, for his morning cocktail. The Lounge was just a couple miles from the Depot. He'd have four or five cocktails. Then it was off to the Depot for the rest of the day. I started meeting him at the Lounge at 6 am, every day. I didn't want to miss any of the action. After a couple hours we both drove (drunk) to the Depot to finish the day.

Star Wash had grown into a pretty profitable business. It would have even more lucrative if I wasn't spending so much time and money in the bars. I had two trucks, and employees out working the routes. I ran the company, by cellphone, from the bars. There wasn't much competition because there wasn't anybody else doing what I was doing. I could flake on customers without much repercussion.

I buddied-up with the other all-day drinkers. There was Frank, who owned a tortilla distribution business. Bill and Dierdre were a couple from New York. You could tell by their accents. Bill was about six feet tall, with dirty blonde hair, and a receding hairline. He was missing a pinky, so everybody in the bar called him 'Pinky.' Bill was a real jokester.

Then there was Corky and his girlfriend, Cindy. Corky was nearly six feet tall and a little over weight. His movements were slow and deliberate – but mainly just slow. He laid tile for a living, and his workday didn't start until 10 am, so he usually hit the bar around seven. His girlfriend Cindy was a bit strange, and kept to herself. She seemed to want to keep their relationship low key. Maybe she was married or something. That bunch became my crew.

CHAPTER 7: VERONICA

My life fell into a dull and drunken routine. Day after day I woke up with a hangover and red eyes. I'd go straight to the Lounge to visit Eddie. *Did I really write visit?* Let me rephrase that. I'd go straight to the lounge to *drink with* Eddie. After an hour or two, I'd head over to the Depot, to hang out with the other aimless sots.

I remember this day like it was yesterday. I walked into the Depot, and standing behind the bar was this beautiful woman, named Veronica. The owner must have just hired her. She was a petite Latino woman with long brownish hair and a very nice figure. That smile of hers just melted my insides.
  "What can I get you?"
  "A vodka and cranberry please."

She seemed very shy. But she had me by the heart-strings at "What can I get you." She didn't seem to care for me at first. But day after day I was there, and she started to thaw a bit. I learned that she had four kids, whose father was out of the picture. Two girls 9 and 14, and two boys 11 and 13. They rented a house about 45 minutes away from the bar.

She was currently involved with a man who lived about two hours away. He was a correctional officer. She told me that she worked three different jobs to keep up with the bills and kids. All three jobs involved bartending in different towns. That poor woman worked so much she never got to spend much time with her kids.

I knew what I wanted the moment I saw her. I'd get her to see things my way – it was just a matter of time. If I could get this woman my life, all my friends would be jealous. Yep, that's what I was thinking. But that boyfriend of hers was gonna be a high hurdle.

Weeks went by while I spent my days trying to get her attention. The fact that I had my own company, that ran on its own, was a feather in my cap. But every time I asked her out, I got the same old run around about her boyfriend. Then one day, to my surprise, she said yes to my dinner invitation. We went out to eat, had a few laughs, and drinks of course. I was literally in love with her. She couldn't help but know it.

In the ensuing weeks I complimented her, called her on the bar phone, and flirted with her. She eventually met with the boyfriend, who she only saw twice a month anyway, and ended it with him. After that, Veronica and I did everything together. Those butterflies of young love were back. And they brought all their friends.

I'd never been happier and more in love than I was then. I drove her to her other jobs, and stayed by her side, constantly. But I had yet to meet her kids or go to her house. My living situation, with Eddie, was about to come to an end. Same ole story.
"Chad, don't this personally, but me and (insert female name here) think it's time for you to blah...blah...blah, blah, blah..."

I was starting to see a pattern in my life. Guy rents me a room – guy meets a girl – guy puts me out. In reality they were just saving their new love interests from my lechery. They would've jumped in my boat. And I would've thrown them back when I was done.

I decided to rent a house on my own. I got a newspaper and went through the 'house for rent' section. I found a perfect three bedroom house, with a pool, just three miles from my shop. I met the owner who was the father of a high school friend. We signed a lease agreement on the spot.

Two days later I was at the bar when Veronica got off. She didn't have to go to another job that night. So we sat and drank as I told her about all my housing drama. I saw a huge tear fall from her eye. Soon she was sobbing uncontrollably.

"Hunny, what's wrong?"

"My landlord evicted us from our house yesterday," she said choking back tears.

I hugged her.

"It's going to be ok," I promised. "Why don't you and the kids move in with me?"

"Ok Chad, thank you," she said wiping her tears.

If you were my 'wingman,' you would have been tapping me on the shoulder, right about then.

"Um, Chad. You do see what's going on here, right?"

But love is blind.

It sounded perfect – *to me*. After all, she was the woman I was going to be with forever. The tears vanished fast and a big smile grew on both our faces. We spent the rest of our evening excitedly talking about the move.

The following day I reached out to the new landlord and told him the news. He was ok with it as long as there were no pets. I got the key and showed Veronica the house. It was close to schools, with a room for her boys, and a room for her girls.

I spent three weeks moving in, while Veronica was at work. After my stuff was all moved, she had me and a friend rent a U- haul to load up her belongings. She had all her stuff stacked in the garage. As we backed in the driveway, the neighborhood kids crowded around the truck asking questions.

But then it dawned on me. *Those are her kids*. And *this* was the first time I met them. Veronica kept a roof over their heads, clothed and fed them, but she wasn't getting any help from their father. It seemed to me that the kids were getting the short end – of a short stick.

It made me think about what my dad did for *me*. And I wanted to do the same for *them*. We stayed in that house for a year and a half. My drinking escalated and I'd taken to gambling on sports, with a bookie, on weekends. Veronica became the manager at the Depot and was able to quit her other two jobs.

Not long after that, I hired a new worker named Teato. He would play a big part in my life story – all though I didn't know it at the time. Teato's parents lived in Mexico. He'd crossed the border to look for work. He found *me* through a mutual friend.

I think Veronica and I were fighting more than we were getting along. She wanted me to be a father figure to her kids. But that just made me drink more. And the more I drank, the more we fought. Often times we would get into it so bad, that I stayed away from home, for days. As bad as I wanted to be the man my father was, I couldn't pull it off. I was too selfish.

I once went so far as to rent an apartment on the side. I was sure it was over for good this time. But we made up just like always. And a friend of mine took over the new lease. The last night in that apartment, Veronica came over and stayed the night. We discussed all the changes we were both going to make, to make our relationship work.

My friend, Frank, the tortilla distributer said I was crazy.
"Man she got four kids. Have you lost your mind?"
I just laughed it off. Veronica was putting up with my drinking. She even covered for me. Veronica's family had lots of family functions. We attended at them, often. I always felt out of place because I was the only White person there. But mostly I felt out of place because I was the only one who drank, to get drunk. I would disguise my vodka in tumbler's full of Gatorade. Nobody ever questioned it, and Veronica always played along.

But the truth was that the whole family knew I was an alcoholic, and that there was vodka in every cup I drank. They put up with me because I made their daughter happy, and took in her kids. I thought that made me a good man.

But I was a sick man, in denial. Alcoholism is a spiritual malady. A dis-ease, that tells you, you don't have a disease. There is no hope of treating the dis-ease, without addressing the spiritual malady. But good luck trying to figure that out on your own, while more-or-less insanely drunk, every waking moment.

CHAPTER 8: MARRIAGE HAZE

After living with veronica for a little over a year, we still fought all the time, over the smallest things. But mainly *her* kids and *my* drinking. When I met her she had a late model car. I never asked her anything about it – why would I? One night the police showed up at our house. They took her car. It turned out that belonged to someone else, and they had reported it stolen. She told them it was a deal gone bad, so she didn't get arrested. I didn't ask any questions because I was drunk off my ass. That night was all just a blur.

The next day I went out and got her a another car, using my good credit, but she had to make the payment. Veronica was always good for her word. But she had never established credit. That's where I came in. There wasn't much I wouldn't do for Veronica. And I would never cheat on her, or so I thought.

On December 23rd, 2003, I was sitting on my usual stool at the Lounge, after a long day of my usual drinking. The Christmas spirit was in the air, and I had a good buzz from a day full of cocktails. Out of nowhere, I got this bright idea that maybe Veronica and I should get married.

I was sure she'd be pleased, and maybe even stop busting my chops about drinking. I made an appointment to see my friend, Danny, at the Diamond Mine Jewelry Store. He called me while I was at the bar the next day.

"Hey, Bro. You're late for your appointment."

I had forgotten all about it. But didn't want him to know that so I hurried off to meet him. The idea of proposing was starting to sound even better. I figured it would make my home life happy, and our love life all good.

So I picked out a ring and bought it.

"What size is her finger, bro?"

"I don't know. I haven't thought that far ahead."

"Really? Ok."

"Tell you what, Danny. I'll bring it back later to have it sized."

"Whatever you say, boss. The customer is always right," he laughed.

I went back to the bar to show all my friends what a great guy I was.

When I got home from the bar that Christmas eve, I shower and changed. I marched straight into the kitchen, and got down on one knee, before I changed my mind. And I proposed to her. I had no idea what I was getting myself into. But I should've know because of the example my dad set.

"Um – Babe. You know I love you," I said humbly but awkwardly. "Will you marry me?"

"Oh yes, Chad. Yes, yes, yes!"

Tears streamed from both our eyes. And we agreed to love each other into a great marriage. That night us and the kids went to her sister's house to make tamales. Veronica showed off the ring I'd bought. Everyone else in her family already had solid marriages. Maybe they saw what we had yet to see. Their blessing was half-hearted, at best. I wasn't Hispanic, *and* I drank too much. But mainly – I drank too much. In other words, I was an uncultured drunk. In better words, a raging alcoholic.

As soon as the holidays passed, Veronica started making plans for the wedding.

"What colors do you like, Chad?"

"Oh, I don't know, sweetie," I lied. "You decide."

The truth was that I didn't care.

"What about the cake?"

"I don't have time to talk, right now."

"We should get married at my parents' church. Would that be alright with you, Chad?"

"It's your wedding, Veronica. Why are you asking me?"

On, and on she went – until,

"Should we serve alcohol? I mean...there'll be kids there. And you know how you..."

"I've never been to a wedding that didn't have alcohol. We gotta serve alcohol. Here – grab a pencil. Let's make a list."

I just wanted all the pestering to go away so I could continue my alcoholic life style. And then one day it finally hit me. *I'm really gonna be married. What was I thinking?* A lot of my friends from the bar kept saying I should get a prenuptial agreement.

"Make sure you get a pre-nup, man."

"Yeah, Chad them chicks will take you to the bank."

"There is no... what's the word?"

"What word?"

"You know. There is no...something, something...like a woman's scorn."

I got the picture – if it wasn't *true* love, there'd be lot of problems. What I *didn't* get, was a prenuptial agreement. I mean...that's like asking your bride to let you take out marriage insurance. The closest I could come, was to act on the following advice.

"Buy a house, before you get married. That way, it's not community property."

I started the process. I was self-employed, so I easily qualified for a 'stated income' loan. I just needed to find a house that was big enough for me, and my newly acquired family; with a payment I could afford on my own – in case something ever went wrong. I found a beautiful single story home, on a corner lot, with four bedrooms and a non-permitted bonus room in the garage.

The house had a white, 4-foot-tall, wrought iron fence around the front yard. It had a pool in back that was surrounded by King palms. It was awful close to being the perfect house, with the proverbial white picket fence. Veronica loved it. The seller accepted my first offer.

But I needed to get my deposit back, from the house I was renting, because I needed it to make the down payment. I went through the rented house with the refund checklist. Oh my God...everything was broken. The boys' room was a wreck. There was writing on the walls and the carpet was stained. Then there were damaged walls and fixtures from my drunken rants. But I couldn't see my part. All I saw was the damage caused by the kids. To keep the peace, I just fixed and painted whatever needed it.

I do believe alcohol helped me to keep my mouth shut when I wanted to go ballistic over the what the kids had or hadn't done. But alcohol also hid *me* from *me*. Without one seeing one's own faults, there can be no healing. I was in total and complete denial. It didn't help that I got most of the deposit back. It only made me feel (and act) more self-righteous.

We closed escrow with two weeks left on the old lease. I spent those last days moving furniture from one house to the other in my Dodge 4x4. I stopped for a cocktail with each trip. And I carried one between my legs when I left the bar. My friends from the bars helped, and I repaid them with liquor, while Veronica worked all day at the Depot.

I forgot all about the wedding. Can you believe that? The utopian bliss of the marriage proposal had worn off. We were back to fighting. But I hid the depths of my anger for the sake of completing the move. She hid hers, I guess, for the sake of her kids. But even those concessions were starting to wear thin. We ended up fighting, full time, over the usual stuff – my alcoholic behavior. I wasn't even showing up at my office anymore. I lived only for my own pleasures – drinking, smoking cigarettes and gambling. But boy did I play the victim.

We quelled our anger, or stuffed it, as the wedding approached. All the while my friends from the bar discouraged the whole idea.

"Getting married to a woman with four kids is crazy," my best man, Frank warned.

And my groomsmen all felt the same way.

"She's playing you for a sucker, Chad."

"She's marrying you for the money."

"All she really cares about are her kids."

The wedding, and reception, were both held at the Green River Country Club golf course. And it was all just a blur. I honestly couldn't even tell you who was there. But I do remember my friend, Dave, who owned the aluminum extrusion company. He got sloppy drunk at the reception and his wife had to help him to their car. I didn't even remember most of the ceremony. I was pretty much in an alcohol induced coma for most of the day.

We were to fly out the next week for our honeymoon in Cancun, Mexico. All our friends from the bar were going to go too – like some kind of mafia movie.

While on our honeymoon in Cancun, we (meaning *I*) really enjoyed the inclusive all-you-can-eat/all-you-can-drink resort. I was in heaven. But my new wife wanted to do this excursion trip, and go here and there, trying different foods and taking in the sights. I wanted nothing to do with any of it. All I wanted to do was drink.

Thank God we had all our friends there to keep her off my back. All I was interested in doing was sitting at the pool bar, and drinking all day, while enjoying the view of the ocean.

I told you earlier that Veronica was stunning. But let me break that down for you – or (in seminar speak), let me unpack that statement. So I'm sitting in the pool, at the swim-up side of the pool bar. What was I doing? Probably drinking and bragging about my made-in-the-shade life. When out walks this curvalicious bombshell, in a string bikini, with a see through wrap.

And every gaze was fixed upon her – Veronica. I could tell by the facial expressions around the pool, that every man wanted to have her, and every woman wanted to *be* her. Now, I was already four sheets to the wind, but I hurried up and claimed her.
"Hey, babe – over here."
She dropped her wrap by the side of the pool and slid in the water beside. My own friends had a hard time not drooling.

After a couple cocktails, on her part, and few *more* on my part, she slipped me the honeymoon cue.

"I'll be waiting for you inside. Don't be long."

We (I) prided ourselves on being a good looking couple. She was an olive-skinned beauty. And I was...well I was 'The Chad.' But I was only the Chad if I stopped drinking at the *sweet* spot – if you know what I mean. Right then, I was basically plowed. So then, my buddies gave me the honeymoon cue.

"Go get her tiger."

I stumbled to the room and tried my best to open the door with the hotel key card. Veronica heard me fumbling and unlocked the door. And there stood the girl of every man's dreams, in a curve-fitting red negligee. *Take her down Chad*, is what I thought. What I *did*, was fall backward on the bed. I wanted to take her down alright. But I saw three of her – all swirling together in my drunken field of view. And all three of her were pissed. I passed out while trying to figure out which one to reach for.

That was a bad night – really bad. I had to make it up to her. *And*, to myself. I never even tried to pace my drinking, but the next day I did. That evening – same scenario. Only this time, Veronica wore a conservative one-piece bathing suit. I guess she had low expectations. This time, I gave the cue.

"Let's go back to the room, baby," I whispered softly in her ear. "I've got something you need to see."

I led her to room 449 and slid my key card through the lock. I searched my entire being for the proper attitude. It needed to be somewhere between "baby let me slap that ass," and "darling I love you." I never did find the right words. All I can tell you is that I *laid* her down, *peeled* that one-piece off her like a tangerine, *opened* her up like a 7/11, and *licked* her up off the floor.

We slept in the next morning. The pool bar was already open when I arrived. I didn't even gloat. It had been a perfect lovers' concerto.

Every day after that, I got plastered during the day, and passed out by 8 pm. I was back at the pool bar first thing in the morning for cocktails. Our friends left two days before we did.

I went on the occasional excursion, just to keep Veronica

happy. But what I really wanted was for her to shut the hell up and let me drink. I couldn't wait to get back to the hotel and the pool bar.

On our last night in Cancun I knew that I needed to step up my game. I actually stayed up past eight, to take Veronica for a walk on the beach. I remember walking down the concrete stairs for the one and only time. They had just rinsed the sand off the concrete steps that led to the beach. The pool bar was closed, so my cocktail was in real glass from inside the hotel. On the third step I slipped on the freshly watered concrete. My cocktail glass fell and broke. I came crashing down on the glass, and sliced open my right arm.

I was in a panic and there was no one around but my wife. Blood was everywhere and I was screaming in pain. We got up and I was able make it to the hotel lobby, where we were met by staff with first aid kits. All I cared about was a new cocktail – extra strong. So I sent my to bride to *fetch* me one from the hotel bar.

The staff finally got the bleeding to stop and patched me up. We went back to our room. That last night was long a silent. I played on Veronica's sympathy. I was good at that. The next day we boarded our flight home – after spending our last few hours at the pool bar. And still I didn't realize what a jerk I'd been. I never even gave my poor bride at chance at happiness.

The flight home was long and awkward. I couldn't wait to get back to my own bed – and to the local bar, where I was sure I would be missed and coddled. I could probably get a lot of free drinks when they saw my arm and heard the story.

CHAPTER 9: NEWLYWEDS

Now here is where things got interesting – as if it wasn't already so weird that I wanted out. In other words, it was all *her* fault. We made it through the wedding and the honeymoon and finally settled into our new home. Although there was still a lot of arguing, we all made the best of it. We dealt with each other's attitudes in hopes that love would still conquer all.

I patterned my life around the same old schedule. Every day I got up and showered, then kissed Veronica goodbye. Then, straight to the Lounge for a couple cocktails and talks with the local drunks. I stopped by my shop/office for a few short minutes, just to check on things before heading to the Depot, where I would spend most of my day.

Veronica usually got to work, at the Depot, before I arrived. But she didn't know I was going to the Lounge every morning. For all she knew I was at work. I mean, I *could've* been at work. And I should have been at work.

I talked and laughed all day. That was my life. I considered it a charmed life. After a day at the bar, I went home and sat by the pool, watching the TV that I mounted under the patio cover. There, I'd drink cocktails and smoke cigarettes before I ate whatever she cooked for dinner. That's it – that's all. Then I went to bed. My daily routine didn't change much, except on Sundays.

Sunday's were very interesting. I'd wake up and head to the kitchen to pour a glass of orange juice and wait for Veronica to come out of the bedroom.

"Good morning, babe. Give me a kiss."

She was always happy to see me with straight orange juice in my glass. But little did she know, I would go out to the garage, and pour vodka into my orange juice. Then I'd cook biscuits and gravy for the family, and for a few of older men at the local bar.

I'd package up two or three portions, in throw-away Tupperware bowls, making sure the kids were fed before I left. Funny thing – I never ate any of the food I cooked. It was just a weird habit.

"I'm off to bar Veronica."

"Ok, hurry back Chad, we have a big day planned."

I drove to the Lounge to deliver my food and have a few cocktails. I had to drink them fast because I knew Veronica was watching the time. She was the managing bartender at the Depot, and took on a side-job at a bar not far away. But Sunday was her day off. She used that off-day to try to reform me. And she watched me like a hawk. Even if she did question my activities during the week, I could lie to keep the peace. But Sundays she planned our entire day – together.

51

CHAPTER 10: BREAKFAST CLUB

This is a story I thought for sure I would never tell. It was Sunday morning and I made breakfast for my normal deliveries at the bar. Veronica and I had plans to meet my friends for brunch, to celebrate a raise that our friend, Bill, had gotten the previous week. I was in a hurry to get back because Veronica was getting ready.

I dropped off the food and sucked down three cocktails. I raced home and pulled in our driveway honking for Veronica to come out.

"Can't you ever be on time, Chad?"

"Sorry, I had to help Charlie with his cell phone. He couldn't call out."

"So why didn't you just him we had things to do. You could have looked at it later. Why can't you ever put your family before the guys at the bar?"

We drove to the restaurant to meet our friends. Well, they were really more like my friends. We were seated with two other couples, at a big round table. I didn't waste a second.

"Champagne all around. And keep it coming."

"My God Chad, it's only 9 am."

"Please don't start on me, Veronica. I'm not in the mood for it."

We all talked and laughed about all things in general. But I could tell by the look in Veronica's eyes that she just wanted to get the whole thing over with and go back home.

She knew that the only way to get us to stop drinking was to get us to the food. She made the move first.
"Well, guys, I'm starving let's go to the buffet line."

As we entered the back room where the buffet tables were set up, there was all kinds of different foods. I saw Veronica look at Bill's wife, Dierdre.
"What are you having, Dee?"
"I think I'll have a salad. How about you?"
"Salad sounds great."

All the guys marched right past the salad bar and went straight for the breakfast spread. As I got my plate, my friend Frank looked at me.
"What looks good to you?"
"Fettuccine Alfredo," I smiled.
I knew that it would be soft and smooth, and I wanted to save room for more drinks.

Everyone was busy filling their plates. I used the tongs to pile my plate high with fettuccine noodles. I scooped a large spoonful of sauce and spread it over my noodles. It was dripping off the side of the plate, so I grabbed some bread to wipe it off, and headed back to our table. It was Sunday, and Veronica was out to teach me manners.
"Is that plate full enough, Chad? Better be careful."
"I'm fine. Would you please stop nagging me."

I walked extra slow back to the table because I felt Veronica's eyes burning a hole in my forehead. The last thing I needed was to trip, or drop my plate, and have Veronica scold me for having too many cocktails.

When everyone finally sat down to eat, I jumped up and grabbed the that ice-cold champagne bottle. After all – it was all you can drink.
"Refills anyone?"
I saw a look of disgust on Veronica's face, as she shook her head from side to side, and rolled her eyes.
"Yes!" everyone shouted between bites.

I grabbed my fork and dug into my noodles. It tasted kind'a funny.

"What's wrong, Chad," Sandy asked. "Is it bad?"

"No I," I lied. "A little cold, but fine."

I finally realized that I'd poured waffle batter over my noodles instead of Alfredo sauce. I knew that if I revealed the mistake, the whole table would burst out in laughter – except for Veronica, of course. She would immediately accuse me of drinking too much and cut me off from having anymore champagne.

Everyone else enjoyed their morning, as I quietly choked down those cold, waffle-battered noodles.

On the ride home Veronica asked:

"So, how was your breakfast?"

Did she know? I couldn't ask her if she knew.

"It was good," I answered, still wondering if she knew.

"And how was yours?"

"Not bad."

My stomach was feeling pretty upset, so a nice nap on the couch was in order. It took all I had, to keep from tossing my 'cookies' all over the couch. I never spoke a word of that incident until now. To this day, I still don't know if she knew.

CHAPTER 11: CHRISTMAS

We managed to make it to the first Christmas, in our new house, as a married couple. Our house was on Ginger Bread Lane. That just sounds like Christmas; doesn't it? The whole street was decorated to the max. People came from far and wide to see our displays. The local paper even did a write up every year about the street. As a tradition, the decorating started on the day after Thanksgiving. By Sunday night, every house was complete.

Our house was on a corner lot, at the entrance to the street. I had such an ego. I made the whole thing a competition. And I was going to make sure that my house stood out from my neighbors. I hired electricians to run wires under my house, and had them run all the outlets to three switches in my garage. I put up so many lights and decorations that you couldn't even tell that there was a house under there at night.

I draped ice-cycle lights all the way around that four-foot wrought iron fence. And all the trees and light-posts were wrapped in lights. I had so many mechanical features in the yard that it looked like the Disneyland electrical parade. I even painted a golf cart red, and put it on the lawn, with a plastic Santa in it.

I put a red plastic sleigh on the roof, with a light-up Santa in it. A team of mechanical reindeer completed the effect. I was on the roof, running the last of the wiring, when Veronica came outside.

"Get down from there, Chad!"

"I'll fine. Stop trippin."

"You're not fine. You've been drinking all day."

I didn't listen. I drank like that all the time.

"I know how to hold my liquor. Shut up before you jinx...Ahhhhh!"

I landed across a tree branch. The tangle of multicolored lights kept me from sliding off. The light-up Santa hung from my ankle.

On the evening of the first lighting, Veronica called my cell phone.

"Are you almost home, Chad? You know it's gonna be dark in twenty minutes."

"I'm almost there," I lied.

I got home two hours later – drunk off my butt. I stumbled to the garage and flipped the three switches. Then I passed out on the front porch while carloads of Christmas light gawkers drove down my street.

As if me drunk on the porch wasn't enough. I had the nerve to put on a Santa hat and pass out candy canes to the children in passing cars. Our house, *and me*, were the talk of the neighborhood. We were *some* spectacle. But all Veronica wanted was a husband that didn't drink so much – and a normal life.

CHAPTER 12: CARELESS WITH LIFE

Our first holiday season was over. We survived it with a precious few pleasurable moments. I took down all the decorations and it was back to our normal life. The problem was that nothing I did was ever normal. Over time I learned to do small things that kept Veronica off my back. One of which was taking her to her favorite restaurant. But we always stopped at the Depot on the way.

"What time is our reservation, Chad."

"Not for another hour."

"Well I guess we'll have to go to the *stupid* bar and have a couple."

I planned all of our activities around plenty of bar stops. And she didn't *seem* to care as long as she got where she wanted to go.

We went back to Cancun too. This time we brought her children. What a great way to keep her occupied, while I spent all day at the pool bar. The kids had fun too. Veronica ran back and forth from our room to theirs, trying to keep tabs on everybody. Between the five of us, we ran her ragged.

We settled in back at home after the trip. And Chad thought...wait, don't you hate it when people speak of themselves in 'third person?' But anyway, Chad thought: *hmmm...wouldn't it be nice to have a brand new Chevy H2 Hummer?*

I knew that if I told Veronica, she would immediately say no, and that would be *that*. I left the bar one afternoon while Veronica was working.

"I'll be back in a few, Veronica."

"Where are you going?"

"I gotta run by the shop. Teato has something to show me."

I snuck off to the dealership to have a look at the new Hummer. The sticker price was $55,000. The salesman reeled me right in.

"Five thousand down and it's all yours."

I thought of how important I was going to look, with a new H2, when nobody else town had one (yet). My truck was *only* a year old. But I figured I would sell it and get out from under the payment. And I would find a way to come up with $1100 a month for the H2. Not clearly thinking the whole thing through, I went ahead and bought it. I had my friend drive my truck back to bar and I drove the H2.

I walked back in the bar beaming from ear to ear. Veronica glared at me.

"Do you think I'm stupid or something, Chad? You haven't spent that much time at the shop since we met. So where were you, really?"

I grinned.

"Go outside and look what I bought."

She didn't speak to me for three days. Until:

"How the hell are *we* going to pay *your* new truck?"

"I'm selling the 4x4. It'll be fine. I promise."

I talked her into going with me for a ride around the block to check out the new vehicle.

"My company is paying for it," I told her. "So it doesn't matter."

"Chad," she answered thoughtfully. "You *are* the company. That means *we're* paying for it. Now that we're married, we need to make choices together."

I polished up my 4x4 and sold it. I was contacted by a refinance man, Harry Tucker, who told me I should consider using equity from my house to buy down the loan on the new truck. At first I hesitated – only because I didn't want to leave the bar to meet him. But after consideration, I thought to myself, *I can pay off a lot of things and lower my house payment at the same time.* So I got on the phone and called him. We were to meet the next day.

Mr. Tucker's office was decorated with cheap paintings and velvet wallpaper. A chill ran up my spine. A feeling of being taken advantage of raced through my mind. His secretary looked at me and smiled.

"Can I help you?"

"Yes. I'm Chad Reynolds. I have an appointment with Mr. Tucker."

"Have a seat, Mr. Reynolds. Harry will be right out."

Tucker walked into the waiting room and reached out to shake my hand. I extended mine.

"Hello Mr. Reynolds, it's nice to meet you."

"Hello Harry," I replied while shaking his hand.

The two of us walked back through the waiting room doors and took seats at his conference table.

"I have reviewed your file, Mr. Reynolds, and we can help in a big way."

"Go on," I said.

He explained the advantages of refinaning my house to pay off the Hummer and a few credit cards.

"It will lower your house payment, substantially."

The first thing that came to my mind was that $1,100 a month Hummer payment. *Wow.*

"Let's make it happen!"

After the meeting I drove back to the bar with mile-wide smile on my face.

"Get the house a round!" I shouted.

I looked at Veronica as I spoke, and watched as she rolled her eyes and shook her head. She'd just got through telling me that we needed to make decisions together.

The following week as I sat on my barstool at the Depot, my phoned rang. As always, I ran outside and answered it.

"Star Wash, can I help you?"

"Hello Chad, it's Harry Tucker."

"Yes Harry. How can I help you?"

"Everything's going fine, Chad. We just need to add your wife's name on the title, because we're using her income as collateral. And it won't change the tax write-off."

I licked my greedy chops.

"That's fine with me," I said with a smile.

After all, we were gonna be together forever.

Veronica went along, of course. Her name would be on the deed to the house. And she'd get to pay off her credit cards. It was a win-win situation. I paid off my Vehicle, and both our credit cards. We had a lower house payment, and I even got to skip a month's payment. It freed up a lot of money for other things – more drinking and less work. I thought the whole deal would make Veronica happy. She wasn't.

CHAPTER 13: HOSPITALS

The days seemed to fly by. Time was slipping way – slowly but surely. And my drinking got worse and worse. By the next Thanksgiving and Christmas season, I was hiding much of my drinking from my wife. Every morning, I made a tumbler full of vodka and Gatorade before I even left the house – to go to the bar.

My appetite was nonexistent. If I ate all, it would be a pickled egg, chips, or a Slim-Jim from the bar. When I checked in on my employees, at job sites, they told me to go away because I reeked of alcohol. Teato feared that customers would smell it, and some even did.

The life I had grown so proud of had turned into a drunken nightmare. That goals I'd had just a few years earlier became a distance and foggy memory. On occasions I would get up in the morning, get dressed up in nice clothes, and tell Veronica and my friends that I had a big business deal.

Then I'd drive to a bar in another city, and kill a few hours drinking, just to return to the Depot and brag about landing another big car washing deal. I was delusional. My whole life was an illusion.

My life was slipping away. And all I could do about it was drink enough to endure the agony of the failure I'd become.

Eventually, even *that* stopped working, All Veronica could do was watch me drown in my own pathos. When she turned her focus to saving her children, I sabotaged her effort.

I went so far as to put sugar water under the beds to draw ants, and then feign anger.

"Look at all these f'ing ants. I thought you told them not to eat in their rooms."

I made a few attempts at 'going on the wagon.' I had to stop for Veronica's sake, and for our marriage's sake. I tried cutting down, switching from vodka to beer, not drinking at home, not drinking in the morning, not drinking at night…on and on, till there was nothing left to try. I literally couldn't stop drinking to save my life.

Another year passed and we made it back around to the holiday season. It was Thanksgiving and I gave thanks (and drank) all day, just like my mother taught us. I knew that the next day we'd start decorating the house again. I was so excited that I even went to bed early that night.

The next morning, I opened my eyes and stared blinking, through a foggy haze toward the foot of our bed. My wife stood there crying. Just staring at me with mascara running down her face. And alongside of my bed, stood firemen in yellow 'turn-outs.' I was confused. The firemen kept asking me stupid questions.

"What day is it?"

"Who's the president?"

I was unable to respond to their questions and started to grow very angry. I sat up and tried to push aside the firemen, and climb out of bed. But as soon as I stood up, my legs collapsed from under me, and I fell to the floor. It was as if my legs were made of rubber. That got Veronica crying louder and screaming at the firemen.

"Please? Please help him?"

"We're trying, ma'am."

They kept saying they wanted to take me to the hospital so they could run tests. I refused, at first. But then I started thinking ahead. I knew there would be absolutely no drinking that day, or the ones to follow, if I didn't go. I laid there in shock as the firemen helped me onto the gurney.

When they wheeled me outside, I noticed how warm our house had been, compared to the brisk air outside. As I looked around, I saw police cars, fire trucks and ambulances. My neighbors goosed their necks trying to see what had happened to me. And I could hear the whisperers.

"I knew all that drinking would catch up to him."

"His wife is so pretty. You'd think he stop for her."

"He's a menace to the neighborhood."

And there I was. An all grown up Dennis – the Menace to society.

When we got to the hospital they wheeled my gurney passed the intake desk, and put me in a bed behind the curtains, while Veronica took care of the paperwork. It seemed to take forever. But a doctor finally pulled back the curtain and looked at my chart.

"Chad Reynolds?"

"Yes, that's me."

"It appears you've had an alcoholic seizure."

"A what? What the hell is that?"

"Severe alcoholic withdrawal syndrome."

I was in full flight from reality. I thought the doctor had a screw loose or something. But Veronica couldn't help but chime in as she shook her head in disgust.

"See Chad – I told you, you drink too much!"

"So am I gonna be ok?" I asked, as the severity of the situation sank in.

"Yes but you need to slow down," the doctor replied.

But that was sensational news. He didn't say I had to *stop* drinking. I just had to slow down.

He gave me a prescription, for Dilantin, to prevent this kind of thing from happening again. On the way home we stopped and got the prescription filled. As we pulled up to the house, the neighbors, who were outside decorating their houses approached the car.

"Are you ok?"

I lied through my teeth.

"Yes I'm fine. Just a dizzy spell."

I thought nothing of it. I wanted to pull out the lights and start decorating. But my wife looked at me.

"No way Chad. Not today. It's rest time for you."

Veronica promised, later that day, that she wouldn't tell any of our friends or family what happened.

The following day I rolled out of bed feeling great. I called my friends to come over and help me decorate, because I was behind schedule. When they arrived that mid-morning the vodka started to flow. But I waited until afternoon to make one for myself because Veronica was bird-dogging me. I'm sure she didn't want to look like a wet blanket so she didn't say much when I poured my first glass.

The medication the doctor prescribed was like getting a hall pass, to drink as much as I wanted, without ever having another seizure. That night, after everyone had gone home, there was very little complaining coming from Veronica. And by the next day there was even less. I drank with full force as we finished up the decorating. We finished it just in time for the big first-light party that Sunday night.

In January I got a letter in the mail from the DMV. My driver's license was suspended, due to unconsciousness, from the seizure I'd had on Thanksgiving day.

At first I was angry at the hospital for giving my medical information to the DMV. But I later learned that is was just standard policy. After a few drinks with my friends, I didn't care anymore. It was just a dumb driver's license anyway.

CHAPTER 14: MARRIAGE GONE BAD

Heading into our third year of marriage, things just kept getting worse. The kids weren't doing well in school. My health was fading fast. And business had slowed way down. I took my pills every day to prevent of another seizure. Veronica's nagging had gotten worse too.

Everyone we knew was trying to help us in any way they could. We were bombarded with advice on marriage, finances, and child rearing. We eventually contacted a Christian marriage counselor. We took separate cars and to our first appointment. The counsellor, Don, welcomed us into his office.

"Good evening Chad and Veronica. Please, have a seat."

We sat around a big oval table in the middle of his large office. After we explained our situation, he pondered on it for a while. And then he gave us our first assignment.

"Chad, this week I want you to drink as much as you want. And Veronica don't you say a thing about it."

I was very happy with his instructions although I didn't think *she* cared much for them. The week went on and I took my medication like I was supposed to. But I drank more than I ever did. And she didn't say a single word about it.

The following week we went back to see Don, in separate cars again. We gave our feedback for the previous week.

"I see, I see. Now this week, Chad, don't drink at all and

let's see how that plays out."

"You mean slow down right!" I asked anxiously.

"No. I don't want you to drink a single drop."

The smile that bloomed across Veronica's face irritated the crap out of me.

"Fine," I said. Starting tomorrow, right?"

I wasn't about to start this nonsense that night.

"Yes tomorrow will be fine," he said with a quaint smile.

When we left Don's office, she went home, and I went *back* to the bar. Fear raced through my entire being. I knew *for sure* that I couldn't go a whole week without drinking. I didn't know why (or how) I even agreed to it. I grew more angry with each drink. I explained my dilemma to a friend at the bar.

The next day I went straight to the Lounge, just like always. I thought up a plan while drinking my morning cocktails. I told her, of course, that I was at work.

I was as nice and sweet as I could be that day. For the next few days I sat her down and told her that I was a changed man.

"I love you, Veronica. We don't need a counselor to run our lives."

She agreed and was very pleased with me. For a couple weeks things were great and my drinking slowed way down. I know that sounds like the drinking was in control, rather than me. As if my alcoholism was an aging horse, named 'Drinking'.

'When my horse got a little long in the teeth, Drinking slowed way down.'

In reality, the alcohol *was* in charge. And I was just trying to rein it in for a spell.

One evening Veronica left work to head home. I was to come home as soon as I finished my drink. Which meant drink three drinks really fast, in Chad-speak. As I was driving home, I looked down for something, and swerved right towards an on-coming police car. I looked up and swerved back. I looked in my rearview mirror and he was turning around. He turned his lights on. *Oh crap!* I had no insurance, my license was suspended, and I'd been drinking all day.

I was oh so close to my house. I didn't speed up I just didn't stop. He turned on his siren, just as I pulled into my driveway.

I pushed my remote, and the garage door started up the track. Looking back, I guess I thought that if I could run in and close the door, he couldn't get me for drunk driving. Five other squad cars screeched up behind the first – all with their lights on.

I jumped out of my Hummer and bolted for the garage door. The door from the garage to the house flew open. Veronica stood there with her hands on her cheeks.
"Chad, what the heck is going on?"
"Move!" I shouted.
"Freeze! Stop right there!"

I didn't make it to the door. I was swarmed, tackled, and handcuffed – right there on the garage floor. That sickening feeling of incomprehensible demoralization sank into my gut. The neighbors were outside watching my debacle. I came very close to puking all over the back seat of the squad car.

I was charged with evading arrest, drunk driving, driving without a license or insurance. And they impounded my Hummer for a 30 day hold. I was released from jail about 3 am. I used the police station phone to call my wife. She didn't answer. Unfortunately the bars were closed. I ended up walking home.

The next day I borrowed a friends extra car to get around for 30 days. Not a word was spoken at home for a few days. The spirit of disappointment filled the house.

The next month I got my vehicle out of impound, and things around the house went back to normal. I was back into my everyday routine. Then I had another seizure. I was taking my medication, but I guess it stopped working. I was rushed to the emergency room feeling dizzy and confused.

After a few hours, a different doctor than before pulled open the curtain.
"Chad, your drinking too much. Your liver and body are going to shut down on you if you don't quit."

I was in no mood to hear this, but even worse, Veronica heard it. The ride home was completely silent. If something didn't change – by that I mean *me*, Veronica was going to leave me. When we got home, I noticed that her laptop computer was open. She'd been researching rehabilitation facilities.

I was in no position to argue. I did whatever she suggested. She found this place called 'The Ten Acre Ranch Rehabilitation Center.' The pictures of the place made it look like a luxury resort. Within a few days we were on our way there. By this time I was feeling better, and able to put up a little fight. But Veronica was clearly calling the shots..

When we arrived at the 'Ranch,' we found the front lawn dead. And the house was in desperate need of repair. The live-in manager took us on a tour. The horses out back were as old and ramshackled as the house itself. Flies swarmed in squadrons around a swimming pool, half full of dirty water and green algae. Veronica and I whispered to ourselves.
"Well this place looks nothing like the pictures," I said rolling my eyes.
"As long as it works, that's all we care about," she replied.

We went inside the house to peruse the amenities. We were unimpressed. The inside wasn't much better than the outside. It hadn't had a spring cleaning in years. The kitchen cupboards were old, faded and locked. The house had three big bedrooms, with four twin beds in each one. The living-room furniture consisted of a couple of old couches. To be honest, I was looking for a reason not to stay, the minute we arrived. Veronica dropped me off with my luggage and split. I signed in for a 30 day stay. *Wow, I'm doomed here in this hell hole.*

I complained about the living conditions from day one. By day three I thought I was cured, and that keeping me there was just cruel and unusual punishment. One of the other *hostages* snuck in a cell phone. I borrowed it late one night when the counselor wasn't paying attention. And I called Veronica.
"Please come get out of here," I whispered.
"Why? You'll be fine."
"This place is disgusting. I love you so much. I promise, this time I'll change on my own."

Being the enabler that she was, she agreed to come and get me the next day. I knew that if she talked to one of the counselors, all my begging from the night before would be for naught. So I packed my bag, and when the time was right I headed for the door. I figured I'd start walking and have Veronica pick me up on the side of the road.

The head counselor just looked at me and asked me to please reconsider. But my mind was set on leaving. I was going to be a free man in 15 minutes.

I walked out and headed down the street. It was only a short walk before my Hummer rolled up, with Veronica behind the wheel. My plan worked perfectly. She didn't get a chance to talk to anybody on the *inside*. I climbed in, and she drove home. On the way she informed me that the rehab hadn't even cashed our five thousand dollar check. She'd placed a *stop payment* on it. I had her stop for soft drinks just to feel freedom.

I felt like I had just been released from prison.
"How do you feel, Chad?"
"Free. Things are gonna be different this time. I promise."

For the next few weeks things were calm, and I only had a few drinks (around Veronica). But when she wasn't around I sucked down drinks, like water. It wasn't long before I was back to the same old Chad again.

After watching me for weeks, Veronica insisted that I get a physical. The results showed that my liver enzyme count was much too high. She went back to the computer and started looking up rehabs *again.* And this time she found one out in the desert about two hours away. I figured this one is only seven days long – so if it would make her happy – and *maybe* teach how to drink like a gentleman, I'm was on board.

We arrived at the facility on a Friday afternoon. The place was on a hill in the middle of nowhere. There were two large living quarters. Each unit housed 20 people; two people per room. There were large bathrooms and showers in the middle of each unit.

The property was probably 15 acres, with rest-stop type bathrooms in the middle of the compound. They had a large covered patio, next to a large swimming pool. The registration office was located in a separate building. In that same building, there was a large dining room that served breakfast, lunch and dinner. There were different meeting rooms all over the property, for drug and alcohol classes, therapy, and group sessions.

There was a detox room, that slept four, in the rear of one of the housing units. They escorted me to one of the detox beds, and watched over me 24 hours a day. Since I was only a seven day resident, I had no privileges at all. No calls out, no calls in, and no visitors. I couldn't eat in the cafeteria without an escort.

The only food I ate the first couple of days was peanut butter and jelly sandwiches, and orange juice with honey, which they kept in the room at all times. The sandwiches stuck to my ribs. The orange juice provided Vitamin C. And the honey replaced the sugar that otherwise came from alcohol. The in-house anti-seizure medication was administered under strict supervision. I thought for sure I was going to have another seizure that first night.

I sincerely believed that I didn't need this place, and that it was full of losers who had no will power. I was in detox, which made me one of the worst of the bunch. But at that time I still couldn't see what everybody else saw. I was doing this for my wife and then going back to drinking like a *normal* person. *What the heck – it's only a week. I might as well make the best of it.*

I asked the counselors a lot of questions while I was there, in detox. I really wanted to know how to lick this drinking thing. All they kept talking about was how to *quit*. Well that wasn't my game plan. I just wanted to drink *normally* again.

I slept a lot those first few days. When my appetite back I was escorted to the dining room three times a day. I felt better with each day that passed. My head *de-fogged*. I was looking forward to my last day. I planned to leave and live my life like a normal person again.

Seven days flew by, and Veronica came to pick me up. I felt like a million bucks. I was bright eyed, clear headed, with a healthy complexion and pep in my step. My counselor was briefing Veronica about after-care, when I arrived at his office.
"Wow, Chad. You look totally different."
I thanked her with a kiss.

For the next few weeks I only drank non-alcoholic beer. Which reminds me of that Picante sauce commercial.

"New York City!?"

I even believed my own lies, because behind her back I always had a couple drinks on the side – as in, not at the Depot because she worked there. One night when I came home she questioned me about my conspicuous absence from the scene.

"How come your not at the Depot all day like you used to be?"

"Oh I work a lot now, that's all."

That was so far from the truth that I almost choked on the words. It was only a matter of time before I was back to my old self, and drinking right in front of her. I convinced myself that it must be God's will for me to drink. Or else, why wouldn't he stop me? As time went on I found myself feeling more and more depressed. I was drinking and chain smoking cigarettes, 18 hours a day – stopping only to pass out for the other six.

I found myself mixing with people who I wouldn't normally associate with. At rehab, they called it seeking out lower companions. I was hanging out with bad crowds, and spending less and less time around my wife. I told myself it was alright as long as I paid the bills.

One night I was hanging out with one of my *new* friends, and two barley legal young women, at his apartment. We drank and drugged while Veronica blew up my phone. I knew she was worried, but I wasn't about to answer the phone.

I hit it off with the 22 year-old woman named Tanya. And we started spending time together. I drank while she smoked meth. And she chauffeured me (in my Hummer) from bar to bar. I was trying to drown out all the shame and guilt. I tried meth a couple times, but it didn't really ring my bell the way it did everyone else's. I was desperate to find *anything* that would fill that hole in my soul.

In no time at all I was having an affair with the 22 year-old. I stayed out for days at a time. It wasn't long before somebody told Veronica. She sat me down one night, with tears in her eyes.

"Chad, I want you to stop seeing that girl and come home, or let's just get a divorce."

I don't know why I was shocked at her ultimatum.

"Ok," I replied. "I *have* been acting stupid and I'm ready to change."

The next day I tried break it off with miss 22. It wasn't easy. Nor, would it be permanent.

"Really, Chad? I was really starting to like you. For *you,* not for your money."

"I think it's for the best," I said with puppy dog eyes. "It's the responsible thing to do. I'm sorry."

She didn't raise a fuss. We both knew it was only temporary. I mean after all, I *was* The Chad. And *she* was miss 22.

So I went back home, and like always things were good for a few weeks. Then back to drinking, drugging, and Tanya. Veronica filed for divorce and had one of her son's girlfriends serve me papers at the bar.

I laughed it off – on the outside, with my friends.

"Another round for the house! Who needs her and her four kids anyway?"

But deep inside it hurt. Bad.

I went home to get my clothes. Her daughter met me out front and handed me a restraining order. I couldn't go within 50 feet of the house.

"What the hell is this?" I shouted.

"My mom got it yesterday. What does it say?"

"It says here that I'm an abusive drinker who has threatened you kids."

There was no answer – just awkward silence as I turned around and left.

The next day I had a policeman escort me into my own home to get some clothes. Over the next month or so I partied harder than ever. There was no one to nag me, or tell me to slow down, or to come home. I spent every night with Tanya. I never even went to work, and I barely ate – until I had a massive seizure one night at a friend's house and was rushed to the hospital. The doctor said to me again.

"You drink too much and you need to stop."

The restraining order ended and I drove home to find Veronica had moved all her clothes out of the master bedroom and into her daughters room. She was going to stay there until she moved out.

"I've already planned to move out, Chad. Me and the kid's will be gone by the end of the week. You can move your things into our bedroom if you want. I really don't care one way or the other."

At that moment, I knew I'd lost her. And I'd lost my self.

CHAPTER 15: DIVORCE

Veronica moved out (somewhere with family) and hired an attorney. Her demands were pretty simple – except in regards to the house. She wanted half. *No way – that's my house*. I replied to her lawyer, stating as much.

'I bought the house before we got married.'
But his response was:
'Yes, you did, but you refinanced it 6 months ago and she went on title.'

I wanted to keep the house, and I even had a couple of alcoholics from the bar rent rooms to help me pay the mortgage. But she wanted 50,000 cash up front, to buy her out, and then the rest of her half at some predetermined date. I didn't have it, so I had to sell the house.

In the meantime business had gotten even slower, and I moved my entire shop to the garage at the house, to save money. I also sold the Hummer and bought a cheaper truck – a 'lifted' Chevy. So I was at least solvent.

She had a friend who sold real-estate. The economy was really booming at the time. He listed and the house and it sold the house within a month.

Now I was faced with finding a house to rent. It had to be

big enough for my two friends who rented rooms. And I needed enough space to run my business. But business was rotten and my health had deteriorated. Even though Tanya said she loved me for *me*, and wasn't in it for the money – it sure seemed like she was. When the money was gone, so was she.

One afternoon I was in the living room drinking my cocktail when a couple of workers showed up to collect some money from me. As Teato was talking to me, the other guy grabbed the keys to my Chevy off the kitchen counter, and took off in my new truck.

I was shocked but I managed to call 911. 30 minutes later they phoned me back stating they had found my truck just a few miles away – totaled in a drainage ditch. The driver fled the scene. If you were to bet I didn't have insurance, you'd win. Now I was without a personal vehicle, but I still had the truck that the guys used for work. The second truck was gone. I had to sell it when business turned south.

One particular morning I awoke feeling ill. I stumbled into the kitchen. My roommate, Bobby, was standing there making a sandwich as I reached for a vodka bottle. *Empty. Dammit.*
"Oh man, Bobby, I'm in trouble. I don't think I can drive to the liquor store. Can you..."
Bobby cut me off.
"Have some hot tea, Bro. And go back to bed."
I shook my head.
"Really? That's your advice?"

He didn't understand that I needed vodka to *live*. Without it, I couldn't do *anything*. I couldn't work, or eat, or walk. I couldn't even sleep without alcohol. But I took his advice, and the tea, and went back to bed.

My bed was a large mirrored-ceiling model, with a high mattress. It took up most of the bedroom. I had another seizure, but no one was there to notice. Veronica was gone, and so was my lifeline. I rolled off the bed and hit my head on the window sill. I landed between the window and my bed, where no one could see me. I was unconscious and bleeding profusely.

Bobby came in the bedroom to check on me before he left

for work. He couldn't see me in bed, but he saw my cell phone on dresser, so he knew I was still home. He searched the whole house before he finally found me lying face down, in a pool of blood. He told me later he thought I was dead. But he realized I was still breathing and called 911.

I did die on the way to the hospital, but the paramedics revived me – Twice. I finally woke up only to see my soon-to-be ex-wife looking down at me. Everyone who'd heard what happened called *her*. She stood over me, shaking her head.

"Are you ever going to learn, Chad? Your parents are on their way. And Teato is at your house cleaning up all the blood."

"Huh? What happened? I was just laying down..."

Just then the nurse spoke up.

"You had a major seizure and rolled off your bed. You hit your head on the window sill. You're lucky to be alive."

When my parents arrived, I could see the pain in my mom's crying eyes. I was so ashamed. *What on earth have I done with my life.* There were friends (that Veronica disliked) outside my room that wanted to see me. But Veronica wouldn't allow them in. She's the one that loved me for *me*.

"I wish I could save you, Chad. I tried. I really tried."

I had to stay at hospital for three days while they hydrated me and stitched me up. I was released with 22 stiches in my lip and head. After I got home I was drinking again in just a few short days. I didn't get a vote anymore. Alcohol was my King.

My health was failing. There was nothing anyone could do because I wouldn't stop drinking. I had dark red eyes. Every morning I threw up bile, because there was nothing else in my stomach. I was fine after I threw up the first two morning drinks. After that I could keep one down. Then it was off to the races all over again.

I saw Tanya, here and there. She was driving me home from family court one day when I had a seizure in her car. At first she panicked.

"What do I do. Oh God, I don't know what to do."

Then she drove to the nearest hospital where they pulled me out of car and loaded me onto a gurney. Tanya found my mother's number in my cell phone and called her. Pretty good for a panicky on-again-off-again side-chick.

Mom came rushing to the hospital where the doctor's explained to me yet again:
"You're going to die if you keep this up."
Mom broke down in tears.
"You're breaking my heart, Son. Why won't you stop? Why?"
But even that didn't faze me. All I cared about was my vodka.

I'd lost interest in all things human: my company, food, women, showering, bills...etc. I made sure I had a gallon of vodka near me at all times. My friends stopped coming around because I was developing what's called a 'wet brain.' In the end, that means 'brain dead' from alcohol poisoning.

Still, and all, I had attracted this woman named Dana into my life. She was like a care taker. She was short and stocky with a manly demeanor. She moved in with me and took care of was left of my business. And she made sure I had a cocktail in my hand, at all times. Escrow was about to close and I had to be out of the house when the new owners were scheduled to move in.

Dana ran off both of my roommates and it was just me and her living there. I was in no way attracted to her but she was curious about *me*. Here I was; this helpless guy. I had money coming, when escrow closed. And I couldn't go five minutes without a drink in my hands. My health insurance lapsed when I stopped paying the premium. I could no longer afford my medication. I don't think my blood alcohol level ever fell below 2.0. And 0.8 is legally drunk.

I had yet another seizure and I was rushed to the hospital in an ambulance again. But this time my senses were all blurred. All I remember was that the air was brisk. The neighbors didn't care anymore. They didn't even come outside. No family or friends ever showed up at the hospital.

When I was coherent the doctor explained what was going on.
"Your nerve's have suffered a great deal of damage. Your

body can't take the punishment anymore. You have substantial liver damage already. Your vital organs will eventually shut down if you keep drinking."

I was released from a wheel chair because of nerve damage. But I didn't have one of my own. My employees, Dana and Teato, were there to pick me up. I could no longer walk. I thought it must be some weird temporary diagnosis. I was sure I'd be fine after a good night's sleep and a morning shower.

When I arrived at home, the first thing Dana did was mix me a fresh drink to get my head on straight. Then I found that my four-wheeled, office swivel chair was perfect for scooting around the house. Though it was a little difficult on the carpet.

The next day came and went and I still couldn't walk. I wasn't in any pain. I just felt like a bowl of Jell-O, from the waist down. But as long as I had my vodka I didn't care. I was about to be a free man, after the divorce was final. And I'd have plenty of drinking money when the house sold. Everything was going to be ok. Ya damn-skippy it was.

Not too long after the divorce was final and the house was sold, I used some of the money to pay $12,000 cash for a 2001 Chevy truck. I rented a beautiful four bedroom newer home, just a few miles from the house we sold. The house had all hardwood floors and a big open concept kitchen with a center island. It was perfect for my office chair to roll around on. I turned one of the bedrooms into a home office.

The house had a large, gated concrete side yard that was perfect for my wash trailer and water machine. I parked my new, used Chevy in the three car garage. I used some of the money to catch up on bills, and put the rest in the bank. A perfect start to my new life as an alcohol induced paralytic.

Dana, who was supposed to be running business, was doing a terrible job of it. She was now in possession of my business checkbook and my bank accounts. Teato didn't like her at all. He kept trying to contact me, but Dana wouldn't allow him access. Things got weirder still. I never saw the light of day. I was just liquored up 24/7.

The money in the bank dwindled away – spent on rent,

utilities, business supplies, payroll, vodka and whatever else Dana siphoned off for herself. I quit smoking for some strange reason. Maybe because I couldn't afford cigarettes *and* vodka anymore.

Dana became more like a warden than a caretaker. She had *all* the keys to *everything* attached to her belt, and they jingled as she walked through the house. She took away my phone and locked the house from the inside. I was a prisoner in my own home. If made any kind of move that was out of the ordinary, she would come hollering.

"What do you think you're doing? You're starting to piss me off, Chad."

I bathed in the tub, once a week, because I couldn't stand on my own. One day, while Dana was in the shower, I made a move for the keys she'd left on the kitchen island. *This is my chance to get help. Move your ass, Chad.* I wheeled over to the counter and grabbed the keys.

I moved as fast as I could toward the front door, but in my haste I jangled the keys. And they made even more noise when I fumbled, with shaking hands, trying to put the key in the lock. I managed to get it in the hole and turn the lock. Just as I was I was about to open the door and scream for help, she came barreling around the corner, naked and soaking wet.

"What the hell are you doing?"

I must have turned white as a ghost. I was scared speechless, as she locked the door and wheeled me into my living room, where she made me a fresh drink, with her naked fat ass in my face.

"Don't you ever do that again! Do you understand me?"

Oh crap. This bitch might actually hurt me.

"Yes. I understand."

Over the next few weeks my checking account almost zeroed out. My parents were worried and finally got a hold of me. I explained the situation to them. And I agreed to go to a two month rehab, if they would help me get rid of Dana.

My dad assured me that it would help me get my health and life back in order. Before I knew it Dana was gone. And my ex-roommates, whom she'd kicked out, were back. I had a week before I was to go to rehab, in the same place I spent seven days. So that week I drank like there was no tomorrow.

CHAPTER 16: BACK TO REHAB

This was the day I was to go to my rehab for two months. My phone rang that morning.

"Hi Chad, it's Mom. I'll be there in 30 minutes."

A part of me had hoped that she had forgotten.

"Ok Mom."

I must have drank a quart of vodka before she got there. I did a quick analysis of my condition, when she rang the doorbell. I couldn't walk, my skin was yellow with jaundice. I couldn't speak very well, and my hands had tremors.

I was looking forward to any help a rehab had to offer. My mom drove my truck so I could take my office chair with me. I had to have it if I was going to move around at all. One of my employees, Dave, loaded the chair in the truck bed and rode out to the desert with me and Mom.

When we got there, my mother went inside and got couple of the staff to come and carry me inside. As they unloaded me, my mother stood on the porch explaining my condition to the house manager, Ray. At first they didn't believe my mother when she explained my condition. The dinner bell rang while she persisted. The escort for the detox clients walked by and did a double take.

"You checking in, Chad?"

I nodded.

"Are you hungry? You want me to bring you a plate?"
I just half smiled.
"No thanks. I'm not hungry."

I should have said yes because I hadn't eaten since God knows when. But food was the furthest thing from my mind. Dave excused himself and went to get my high-back swivel chair from the truck. As he rolled it in, the Manager looked at him.
"What is that for?"
"It's for Chad," Dave answered. "He can't walk."
My mother explained how I used the chair.
"Ma'am," Ray said politely. "We can't let you have that here – for insurance reasons – you know"
"But he needs to get around."
Ray smiled.
"Hold on. I'll be right back."
He disappeared for 10 minutes then walked back in to the office pushing a wheelchair.
"How's this?"
Mom and Dave left, rolling my office chair with them.

Ray helped me from the wooden intake chair, to the wheelchair. *I don't need no wheelchair. I'm not handicapped.* But then it sank in. If I stood up on my own I would fall over. I was shown to my bed in the detox room. I'd been there before, so I knew the drill.

I remembered how good I felt the last time after only seven days. *After two months I'll be a new man.* My first night was rough. Thank God for the system they had in place for the detox bunch. At sunrise, I had another seizure.

I heard a siren before I knew what was happening. The ambulance was there in a hurry. Two paramedics moved me from my bed onto a gurney. I heard people yelling.
"Clear the halls! Clear the halls!"
Residents lined both sides of the hallways, all the way out of the building – like gawkers passing a traffic accident.

My parents met me at Desert Springs Hospital. Different doctor – same bad news.
"Mr. Reynolds listen very closely. You're going to die if you don't stop drinking."

They hydrated me and gave me some Dilantin to help calm me down. A few hours later they released me to my parents, who drove me back to the Ranch. When I arrived a couple of nice guys put me in a wheelchair and rolled me back to the detox room.

The next two nights, I thought I was going to die. I was shaking and throwing up emerald-green bile. I couldn't even hold down water. My skin felt like there were worms crawling under it. I just laid there and moaned. The guy on detox watch just smiled at me.

"Your just detoxing."

What was your first clue, Sherlock?

During the day, I sat in my wheelchair and rocked back and forth. After few days I was able to hold down a few sips of orange juice and honey. I finally ate some whole food and was able to keep it down.

I remained in the detox watch room for five days, before they put me in a two-man dorm room. I felt like an outcast. Even though everyone there had a drug or alcohol problem, they could all walk. *I* felt like they thought I was faking to get attention. Since I didn't receive any special attention, I was late to every hourly change of venue. Everyone else was seated by the time I rolled in.

As the days went on, I became more and more aware of my surroundings. There was a large living room with a TV and couches arranged a horse-shoe shape. The TV was on at night for one hour. But the real treasures were the books, about recovery, that lined shelves around the room.

Every morning it was: up early, make beds, meet under a large metal canopy in the center of property, and sit in a circle of chairs for the reading and morning meditation. After a few moments of silent meditation we'd go around the circle for a quick share. After the sharing was completed we would all go for a walk around the property.

I, of course, just wheeled around the property in my chair, but I did participate. As we ended our walk, we all met in the dining room for breakfast. After that we dove into our daily ranch duties. We were assigned to different chores all over the ranch. We kept the same chore, day after day. The purpose being, to occupy or minds for two hours a day.

Throughout the day we had classes, in groups, to help us understand and overcome alcoholism. Anyone that refused to follow the schedule was asked to leave the institution. They did have a pay phone in front of the main office. But residents had to be there for 30 days before they could use it.

Also, after 30 days, we got to have a visitors on Sundays. After 45 days, we got weekend furloughs, under family supervision.

After a few weeks my appetite came back in full force. Mom brought cases of protein drinks to help me put on some much needed pounds. But there was little improvement in my actions or overall appearance. I was still jaundiced and unable to stand on my own.

One day the head counselor, Ray, called me into his office. To my surprise my parents were sitting there. I hadn't seen my parents for weeks. There was a lot of hugging and crying going on. Ray coughed to get out attention.
"Chad's been here for almost three weeks. Unfortunately, we haven't seen much improvement in his medical condition."
"He looks a little better," my mom proclaimed, with optimism in her eyes.
Ray let her enjoy the moment before he continued.
"We think you should take him to the hospital for a medical evaluation."

Not too much more was said before my parents loaded me into their car and took me to the hospital. When we arrived, they had already had my records from my visit three weeks earlier, when I had the last seizure. The doctors poked and prodded me for a couple of hours. And then sent me back to the waiting room, with my parents.

When he finally came back, the news was worse than any of us expected.
"Chad I'm very proud of you for being sober for 20 days. But your alcohol paralysis has advanced. The nerve damage is irreversible. And you are in a state of decline."
The news came as quite a shock to Mom.

"What exactly are you trying to say?"

I held my breath for his answer.

"Mrs. Reynolds – I can't see Chad surviving another month. But who knows?"

"Are you telling me my son is going to die?" my mother shrieked. "But he stopped drinking."

"It's too little, to late. I'm sorry. I really am."

My hope was destroyed. And I really didn't care. I just wanted a drink.

My parents acted like they didn't even hear the prognosis. As we drove off, I thought for sure they were taking me home to die, but they took me right back to the rehab. I had no strength to argue back. I felt like a wet noodle without much of a brain. They put me back into the wheel chair and wheeled me into the rehab. Residents stared at me like they were surprised that I was back.

Another week and I was actually starting to feel better. One of the residents owned a pharmacy, and had them ship a brand new candy apple red walker, just for me. It had wheels, brakes and a place to sit. So I could sit and roll, or stand and walk. It even had a basket on the front of it. I was ever so grateful and let him know by constantly thanking him.

I felt a *part* of, now that I could at least stand up. I eventual regained partial use of my legs, and actually walked, leaning on the walker. Every day around 4 pm, just before dinner, we had leisure time. There was always a line of people in front of the office for mail call. I was always excited when I had mail from my parents or sisters.

My younger sister, Kim, mailed me pictures of my two nephews. The letter said that they miss their uncle, Chad. I remember just sitting there with a stream of tears running down my face. I had totally blown my life away, and if I ever did recover, I would do things so much differently.

The rehab had an ongoing invite to an annual, AA sponsored picnic, in a nearby park. And, because I now had more than 30 days, I was allowed to go. It was my first time leaving for someplace other than the hospital. There was a softball game. And even though I couldn't play, I got to have a hot dog, and lay in the warm sun, and get some color back in my face.

On the way home from the park I had had a short conversation with the van driver. He looked at me when we stopped at a red light.

"That's the most you've said in four weeks, Chad."

"I feel much better today," I answered with a smile.

Two days later my parents called. They were bringing me to their house for a weekend stay.

"Your dad needs your help clearing up some of your invoices."

"Sure, Mom. Whatever you say. See you on Friday."

We went through the invoices on Saturday morning. My company was barely solvent. It was operating month to month. After paying bills and payroll there was nothing left over. I suspected that I'd drank up all the equity. But I didn't admit to it, out loud.

It was such a blessing for me to be there but I felt like a bother. The room I slept in was upstairs, across the hall from my parents. I guess, so they could keep an eye on me. When I woke up Sunday morning, my parents were already downstairs, making breakfast. My walker was downstairs too. I didn't want to bug them. I wanted to do things on my own. So I crawled from the bedroom to the hall bathroom. I used the towel rack and walls to pull myself up and into the shower.

I dried off, crawled back to my room, and got dressed. I scooted down the staircase, one stair at a time, on my butt. My walker was beside the foot of the stairs, where my parents left it after carrying me upstairs for the night. I pulled up on the walker and walked/rolled into the kitchen.

"Good morning, Mom. Good morning, Dad."

They turned to me with a surprised look on their faces. My dad greeted me first.

"Good morning, Son. You got ready on your own. Good man."

A tear formed in the corner of my mother's eye.

"I knew those doctors didn't know what they were talking about."

And she held me in her arms...for a long, long time.

They seemed to be impressed with my progress. Well, so

was I. I felt a little bit like a normal person for a change. We ate breakfast and then I sat down in front of the computer to resolve some conflicting invoices. I was confused at first. I could barely remember how to add and subtract. There wasn't much of a company left.

That evening my parents drove me back rehab. I was greeted by residence's asking how my weekend went
"Glad to see you back, brother Chad."
With two weeks left at the facility, I was up moving around and my speech was improving. I gained some weight and got my color back. My last days were spent working the 12 steps of Alcoholics Anonymous, and working on relapse prevention.

They tried to find jobs for residents exiting the rehab. But I owned (just barely) my own company so all that wasn't for me. Graduation day was fast approaching. I was about to be released back into society.

Ray called me into his office.
"You know, Chad. Another 30 days would probably be best for you."
"No, Ray," was my answer. "I gotta get home and save my company from going under. But you cured me, Bro. I can't thank you guys enough."
"Chad," he said with a concerned look. "There is no cure for alcoholism."
I shrugged it off.
"Don't worry, Ray. I'll be fine."

When the big day arrived, my parents were there to pick me up. I had big plans for a full recovery of body and finance. My mother had already told my two roommates that there was to be absolutely no alcohol in the house. In response, they drank their fill before they got home.

Man, I sure got around great with that new walker, on those hardwood floors. I stayed sober a grand total of seven days. But then I convinced myself that: *a few wine coolers won't hurt. Besides, vodka was my problem.* I started with a four-pack of wine coolers in the garage refrigerator, so my roommates didn't see them and tell my parents.

I bought a work truck from a guy at the bar who agreed to

carry the loan, himself. But, pretty quick, I fell behind on the payments and he came and repossessed it. My dad loaned me the money to get it back *and* pay it off.

The business hadn't picked up much. But my thirst for wine coolers sure did. One morning I got up and rolled into the garage hoping to grab a wine cooler. *All gone. What the hell?* But there was a warm, half-drunk bottle on the workbench. I went and got a cup of ice. As I picked up the bottle I noticed that there were ants all over it – inside and out.

I poured it on ice anyway and drank it – ants and all. I knew I was in trouble. Within a few short weeks I was back on the hard stuff. People left me alone because it was the holiday season again. Eggnog with a little brandy wouldn't trigger any concern. But I wasn't drinking eggnog with a little brandy in it. I was drinking *brandy* with a little *eggnog* in it.

After the holidays I woke up one morning and looked for my roommates' vodka stash, after they left for work. *Those guys are as bad as me. There has to be a stash around here somewhere.* I found a bottle hidden in the dirty clothes hamper. I only took a couple of swigs a day. They didn't notice – or they pretended not to. I finally started going back out to the bars on my walker. But all the local bars had a pact. No vodka for Chad – only beer. *Curses, foiled again.*

CHAPTER 17: WORSE THAN BEFORE

I thought my life was already spinning out of control. But it just kept getting worse by the day. But as long as I was drunk, I was ok. My utilities were getting shut off, and I was two months behind on rent. So it was safe to say I was in a very dark spot in my life, and I saw no light at the end of tunnel.

I basically pawned my 2001 Chevy truck for 5,000 cash, and picked up a new loan on a 2001 Chevy Tahoe that totaled 13,000 dollars, with a payment of 361 dollars a month. Are you confused? Yeah, well so was I. To this day I'm not sure how I let myself be talked into that. But I did have a little breathing room with the 5,000. I paid past due bills and caught up on my house payment, and before I knew it, the five grand was gone.

Once again my parents got wind of my condition and took me back to the rehab for another seven day 'spin dry.' They didn't seem at all surprised that I was back. I left there thinking that things would be better, just like always. In 30 days I was right back to where I started: physically financially, and spiritually broke.

Teato was never paid on time. The bank shut my account down because of all the overdrafts and defaults. But somehow I always had a few dollars to buy cocktails and cigarettes – even if I had to borrow it from the proverbial Peter, and Paul. You might as well include Mary, from the old folk group: Peter, Paul, and Mary.

It was typical for me to get a phone call from my landlord, when the rent was late. But this time his patience had run out.

"Chad, it's Richard. You know – *your landlord*. You're two months behind on your rent...*again*. Either pay, or move out. I'm serious this time. Pay our quit."

I moved back in with my parents, aaaagain. I put whatever *stuff* I had left in a 100 dollar a month storage unit. I parked my work truck and trailer in a 50 dollar a month dirt lot, north of town. Both the lot and storage added up to less than two days, worth of drinking. But I was hard-pressed to pay them.

One day I found a big red lock, on my storage unit, with a note saying:

ACCOUNT SERIOUSLY PASSED DUE – NO ADMITTANCE

My trailer storage would be months late too, but the man was an acquaintance of mine. And he just listened to my lies. I became accustomed to drinking a beverage called 'Sparks.' It was an easy-to-drink orange flavored malt liquor. It didn't really look like an alcoholic beverage, so the police would never think twice about it, if I got pulled over with a can between my legs.

My parents' house was in Riverside. Every morning my father would get up at 5 am to shower for work. As soon as he left I would come downstairs and have a drink before I took off for Corona. I didn't want to have another seizure, so I always stayed liquored-up. Having it my bedroom and in my truck was a must.

My friend from the bar had this 1999, Chevy 1500 truck he was selling. It would be perfect for towing my wash trailer. He was willing to carry the small loan for me, so I bought it.

I developed a semi-functional routine, where I actually showed up at my company. I'd stop on the way into Corona for a Sparks. That would steady my nerves enough to make it to the Lounge, where I'd suck down a few beers before meeting Teato at the dirt lot. And for the first time in years, I did a few mobile washes with my own hands. I'd hit the Depot before I left Corona.

Veronica still worked there. Deep down inside me, I still loved and cared for her. It was important to me, for her and all my old friends to know that I was still *the Chad.* I pretended as best I could.

There was a local bar by my parents' house. You already know I had to stop there to drink enough to be cordial with my folks. No one there knew of my drinking history, so I could order hard liquor without raising eyebrows.

At home, my mother called me down for dinner.
"Chad dinner is ready."
"Be right down."
I'd eat some dinner then go back upstairs to bed. But I set the alarm for 2 am. I would get up, go downstairs and pull out my stashed bottle of brandy. And I drank, alone and happy, until I heard the upstairs shower come on at 4 am. My dad was up. I had 30 minutes to get back upstairs.

I was still a bit wobbly. I no longer used a walker to get around, but I always had it in my Tahoe, just in case. The Tahoe, by the way, was four months behind on the payments. But the bank had no idea where I'd had moved to, so they couldn't reposes it; right?

I heard this noise outside my bedroom window one night. The 'repo' man, from the bank, was hooking up my Tahoe to his tow truck. *How the heck did they find me*? I scurried downstairs as fast as I could but my motor skills were pretty bad.
"Wait a minute, Bro. I paid today."
"You can call the bank in the morning to get it straightened out. But right now I gotta take your truck...*Bro.*"

He was kind enough to let me take out my personal belongings before he towed it off. The next morning I phoned Teato and told him what happened. He drove out and picked me up in his truck, and drove me back to Norco to pick up the Chevy 1500 I'd recently purchased.

The truck was uninsured and hadn't been legally registered,

by me, due to lack of funds. I often stole registration stickers off other cars. If I couldn't find a sticker, I put the paper plate from the dealer back on, to pretend I had just bought it.

That truck of mine never did see more than a quarter tank of gas. I ran out of gas at least twice a week. We kept a one gallon gas can in the bed of the truck for the pressure washer. So *Teato* could walk to the nearest gas station. I made sure I had gas when Teato wasn't with me. *I* couldn't walk more than 10 feet without falling.

I wasn't thinking much about the future. I figured I was gonna live with my parents forever. Lately, I was secretly drinking brandy, while reading a book I stole from rehab. The book, 'Alcoholics Anonymous' was all about people who had drinking problems. *Those poor bastards. How can someone let alcohol control their life.* I sat there crying for the characters in the book, as I sipped brandy, with a splash of eggnog.

I kept the work truck and used it to commute back and forth to work, where I also used it for towing the wash trailer. One morning. I stopped at the local gas station, just like always, to get a can of Sparks for the ride. I pulled out on the street and cracked open my Sparks. I was waiting at the traffic light when I noticed a Highway Patrol car two cars back.

I thought nothing of it. They were probably headed for the freeway to set up a speed trap, or something. But this time it was the '*or something*.' When the light turned green. I proceeded across the intersection. The patrol car got behind. Red and blue flashing lights filled my rearview mirror, immediately. *Damn, not again.*

I dropped my open container behind my seat, and pulled into a parking lot. The officer approached my truck, on the passenger side.
"Do you know why I stopped you?"
"No I don't, officer."
He sniffed twice, and that was all she wrote.
"Have you been drinking?"
"I had a couple this morning. I have this seizure problem, and I have to….well basically…Blah bla blah bla blah….

He opened my truck door. I was hoping the Sparks had been

absorbed in the carpet, because if it hadn't, it was going to start dripping out onto his boot.

"I'll need to see your license, registration, and insurance."

"Yes sir. Just let me find it for you," I said as I pushed things around in my glove box.

"Honk at me when you find them. I'll be in my patrol car."

"Ok," I lied, knowing darn well I didn't have any of it.

In a few minutes he came back to my truck.

"Looks like this is your lucky day," he told me and handed me a ticket.

"Sign it right there," he pointed.

My hands were shaking. I don't know how I managed to sign my name.

"And, Mr. Reynolds. If I see you driving again, I'm going to arrest you on the spot. Is that clear?"

"Yes sir. Thank you sir."

The ticket had the following infractions on it: Driving without registration, driving without a license or insurance, driving while under the influence, a warrant for a previous DUI, suspended registration, stolen registration sticker, and driving against doctor's orders. I parked the truck, concerned that he might radio another cop that had time to take me to jail. I called AAA for a tow to my parents' house.

When I got home, I was a shaking, stuttering mess. I gulped down three beers, while I explained the situation to my mother. And when I finally calmed down, I was ready to drive to Corona. I had to get to the bar and tell others how I talked my way out of getting arrested. I'd have some drinks. And maybe someone would even feel sorry for me, and pay for a round or two.

What I'm about to share with you, is the pivotal point in my path to oblivion. All that time (and I mean for years) I'd been so focuses on my own drinking, that I hadn't even realized that my mom was drinking too. She was so busy, secretly drinking over my drinking, that she developed cirrhosis of the liver.

My father took early retirement to look after my mother. He approached me one evening when I came home.

"Chad, if you're want to continue living here, you're going to have to take your mother to an AA meeting, four nights a week."

Well that was a bombshell. *What kind of crap is this*? *She drank herself sick, now I have to go to AA.* But I took her – four nights a week – *after* I finished drinking at the bar.

For many a night, I sat through those ungodly meetings, staring at the clock. *Oh God, will it ever end?* All I could think about was going to the liquor store on the way home. And here's the kicker. Mom bought liquor for both of us.

We'd stop in a nearby park, and have a few drinks in my truck, before returning home. My dad had no idea, and just thought the meeting was more than one hour. We kept this up until my mother wasn't well enough to go to meetings anymore, because her failing liver made impossible to get around.

CHAPTER 18: FIRST YEAR SOBER

On the morning of September 11th of 2008, I awoke not feeling any different than my usual miserable self. That first can of Sparks was I all that was on my mind. I needed it to settle my stomach and calm the morning jitters.

I got in my truck and took off to my first stop of day – the gas station on the corner. I was feeling a little parched. I mean I was actually thirsty for a cold nonalcoholic drink. I went to the refrigerator door just like always. But instead of sliding open the door for a Sparks, I opened the door next to it and grabbed a Gatorade. I figured I would just stop again and grab a Sparks later that morning. I grabbed a newspaper while I waited in line for the cashier.

The cashier that rang up my Sparks every morning gave me a funny look.
"Will that be all today?" she asked with a smirk.
I was a little surprised myself. But there were plenty more liquor stores between there and the job.
"Yes. Just the Gatorade and the paper."

My nerves were on edge. I was doing something completely out of the ordinary. I paid the cashier and headed out to my truck. I pictured her staring at me as I drove off. I was already second-guessing my purchase. What was done was done, and I continued to Corona.

As I pulled up to the dirt lot were my trailer was stored, I realized that I was actually on time, for the first time in a *long* time. Teato questioned me as soon as I stepped out of the truck.

"What the heck is that your drinking?" he chuckled.

"Gatorade."

He rolled his eyes.

"Whatever you say, Chad."

"I quit drinking," I said, to my own surprise.

"How many times have I heard that story?" he laughed.

"But this time I really mean it!" I shouted

He just shook his head and smiled as we hitched the trailer to my truck. We only had a few jobs on the books for the day. I had become a terrible business owner and only did small jobs to net a few bucks for booze, and to put a few bucks in the gas tank.

When we arrived back at the dirt lot a few hours later, I was shocked that I hadn't even *thought* about a drink all morning.

"Ok, Teato, see you in the morning around 7:30."

"You mean 9 or 10," he chuckled.

"I have an AA meeting in Riverside from 6 to 7 am, and the drive to Corona is takes half an hour. So, Yeah – see you at 7:30."

He looked at me with a smirk.

"I won't hold my breath."

I guess I'd earned his disdain for all the times I'd let him down in the past. My drinking affected his income too. I went to see my friends, *and* to test my resolve. I hadn't been in the bar all morning. Surely my friends and bartender were curious regarding my whereabouts. I greeted the bartender and smiled.

"I'll just have a Coke."

She pour my Coke in silence. So I started the conversation myself.

"Hey guys. Believe it, or not, I haven't had a drink all day."

I don't think they even cared. A buddy, *named* Buddy, made eye contact with my reflection in the mirror behind the bar.

"Good for you, dummy," he growled.

The bartender topped off my Coke, and whispered.

"I'm proud of you."

I didn't receive the praise I'd expected. Maybe they would if I bought them a round. But I didn't. I tipped the bartender a dollar and headed home. After all the times I'd *tried* to quit, the actual *quitting* came somewhat unceremoniously. It was like someone else quit *for* me.

The next few weeks came, and went, a day at a time. My head was starting to clear. I walked with my head held high, and looked people in their eyes, instead of studying their shoes. I hadn't laughed or smiled in years, unless I was buzzed or drunk.

I met Teato at my trailer on time – every day. I filled my gas tank for the first time, in as far back as I could remember. My life turned around, in the first few weeks. At the morning meeting, I shared about a *new* sensation that had come over me. I was overtaken by *sincere* gratitude.

"Thanks guys. Just...really...thanks. This sobriety thing just snuck up on me. I'm as surprised as you are. What would I do if you weren't here to show me how to wear it?"

After the meeting, one of the 'old-timers' shook my hand – and held onto it.

"This is God – doing for you what you couldn't do for yourself."

My parents, and Teato, were in shock. But nobody at the bar gave a rat's rusty rear end. They didn't talk to me at all, now that I wasn't drinking. To them, I'd become an unwelcome stranger. I don't know why it bothered me the way it did. But I got the message, eventually. And I stopped going. Instead I went to AA meetings. There, they were proud of me every single day I (or rather God) put under my belt.

I liked it so much that I started going to two meetings a day. Before I knew it I was going to three meetings a day. And, I was working *five* hours a day. I went to the noon meetings in Corona, because I *worked* in Corona. The friends I met there replaced the friends I used to have at the bar. And there was a huge difference in their caliber of friendship. They didn't want anything *from* me – but everything *for* me.

One night, after the 5:30 pm meeting, I was driving home and felt this odd pain in my stomach. I pulled off the freeway and into the first available parking lot. That unfamiliar pain was hunger. My stomach rumbled. I was having hunger pangs. I had forgotten what hunger felt like. That most basic human instinct was foreign to me. I was parked near one of those gas station mini-marts. There was food in there.

The smell of hot dogs wafted up my nose. That's right – those simple, precooked hotdogs that they kept under the heat lamp, smelled heavenly. I grabbed two of them and covered them with all the toppings they had out on the counter. Then I walked over to the soda fountain and poured myself a nice cold Coke.

There were a few people in line ahead of me at the cashier. As the line grew shorter, my appetite grew stronger. There was only one cashier at first. Then this sweet older lady came out of the back, and opened the other cash register.
"Next."
"Thank you so much," I said as I put my items on the counter.
They were just 50 cent hotdogs, but they represented freedom to me; freedom of choice, freedom of time, and freedom from alcohol addiction.

I wasn't in the truck for 20 seconds before I was wolfing down those hot dogs, with condiments squirting out the end. I gulped big swallows of Coke to wash them down. *Those were the best hot dogs I ever ate*. I drove away knowing that my mom would have dinner on the table when I got home. And another foreign sensation ran through my gut – raw, unadulterated guilt.

I was rapidly approaching a month of sobriety. Emotions and feelings were flooding out my former reality – drowning it. The old me...was drowning, so that the new me could be born. On Monday nights they handed out chips for various links of sobriety. It was important to me, that my mother saw my progress. So I brought her with me to pick up my 30 day chip.

As we sat, the person in charge of chips called out.
"Anyone with 30 days of continuous sobriety?"
I raised my"hand.
"Yes. I do."
I got up and hobbled across room to get my chip. I was still

wearing a knee brace. It took me a while to get there. I was just as proud of *walking* to take the chip, as I was about taking it.

Just as I reached out my hand, somebody shouted.

"I guess we won't be seeing *him* around here anymore."

The whole room laughed because they knew it was a joke. And I common joke, at that. Everyone knew it, but me. *What a jerk, I'll show you.* And that butt hurt feeling kept me sober until I got the joke. By then I liked being sober, and I liked going to meetings.

The group suggested that I get a sponsor and buy a Big Book (A big, blue book called Alcoholics Anonymous). I already had the Big Book, that I'd gotten from the rehab. But I bought another one, just because they said *buy* one. They said I needed to get a sponsor and work the 12 steps.

The first person I approached in was a guy named Donnie. Donnie was a deep-voiced man in his 30's. He sported a neat 'crew cut.' Everything about Donnie was neat and tight. He might have been a former marine, or something. But I didn't ask. All I knew is that he had two whole years of sobriety. So he must've know the secret to this thing. I asked him to be my sponsor.

"Sure. I'll help you."

"Great," I smiled. "What do I do first?"

He smiled back and asked.

"Do you have a big book yet?"

"I bought one the other day, but I haven't started reading it yet."

"Well the first thing you need to do is start reading it, from the first page, and give me call tomorrow."

I'd decided that I wanted this thing called sobriety, and that I would go to any length to keep it. Donnie said read, so I read. If Donnie told me to pick up cigarette butts in the parking lot, I picked up cigarette butts. I washed coffee cups, mopped the meeting room floor, and whatever else Donnie told me to do.

But when Donnie told me I had to start clearing away the wreckage of my past, I had to ask:

"Donnie. What exactly does that mean, in my particular case?"

He laughed. Then he paused, and laughed again.

"Come on, Stretch."

He called me stretch because I was a lot taller than him.

"You *have* warrants and tickets. You *don't* have a driver's license or auto insurance. You're *probably* still ducking bill collectors. Do you owe back taxes?"

I nodded, and he went on. The list was long. He closed with this.

"We'll get started on the steps on Monday. Enjoy your weekend."

He *must* have been a marine. Maybe he still was.

Ok, so first stop – the DUI attorney that I'd stiffed.

"Well, well, I don't believe it," he said as I entered his office.

I shrugged my shoulders and explained.

"Hey, James. Sorry I bailed on you. But I had a problem with alcohol."

"That's usually the case when somebody has multiple DUI's. So what's new?"

"I got sober. My AA sponsor told me I need to get my life straightened out. And..."

"And what?"

"I got another rather lengthy ticket. I'm not supposed to even be driving."

He shook his head and looked at me.

"I think I remember who your judge is. I play golf with him on Wednesday. I'll see what I can do about getting your license back. But in the meanwhile you still owe me money. And..."

"I'm listening?"

"You may have to do a little jail time."

James called me with an update on my case, on Thursday.

"I spoke to the judge."

"Well?" I asked and held my breath.

"No jail time. He dismissed your new ticket and lowered your fine. Pay the fine, complete Alcohol School, and he'll drop all your charges. It impressed him that you were working the steps of AA. He understood that you were making amends for the trouble you caused while you were drinking. He told me to tell you to keep up the good work. Chad?"

"Yeah I heard you," I said with tears in my eyes. "I'll have your first payment next week."

"Thanks Chad. Give it a couple business days, then you should be clear to go to the DMV.

My sponsor, Donnie, called it a God shot. He went with me to the DMV, the following Tuesday. My registration was three years past due. They told me I needed proof of insurance, a smog check, and all my tickets paid in full before they could lift the suspension on my registration. They told me that there was court ordered Alcohol School that must be completed before I could get my license back. I already knew that.

Donnie forbade me to drive until I got it all straightened out. My lawyer told me to get signatures at the meetings for proof that I was attending. Teato, and my dad, helped me out with rides while I followed through on the DMV's requirements.

It took me a couple of weeks, but I finally got all the fines paid, got car insurance, and passed a smog check. I went back to the DMV and paid for my registration. Oh my God. What a relief. Now I just needed to work on getting my license back.

Before I finally completed the Alcohol Class, they told me I had to get a card signed at eight AA meetings. I was going to three meeting a day, so I had that done in three days.

But the day I went to get my driver's license back, the DMV clerk looked up my record.
"We need a medical clearance from a doctor."
I wasn't surprised. But I had yet to learn patience.
"Well no one had ever told me that."
"I'm sorry, sir. But that's what we need. Next in line."

I left there very angry. I immediately called my sponsor from the truck I wasn't supposed to be driving. I hadn't learned integrity yet either.
"I can't believe it, Donny. Now a gotta get a note from my doctor."
"It looks like you had expectations," he answered.
"They could've told me that when we were here two weeks ago."
I was in the middle of my rant, when Donnie stopped me.
"Take a breath, Chad. Keep it simple. Make an appointment with your doctor."

Donnie helped me with simple, common sense direction, like that. God knows *I* didn't have any common sense at the time.

All I knew was that I wanted what I want – when I wanted it.

I made an appointment with the doctor, the very next day. He set me up for a brain scan. I did an awful lot of worrying over things I had no control over. Donnie told me to repeat the following prayer, every time I got frustrated:

God, grant me the serenity to accept the things I cannot change, the courage to change the things I can, and the wisdom to know the difference.

The brain scan came back normal, and I got my driver's license.

Donnie told me to start making a list of the things I wanted to accomplish each day. Day one: go to a meeting, go to work, find a new storage facility, and don't drink. After the morning meeting, I drove to Corona and met Teato for work.

After work I went to the nearest storage lot and signed a contract to lease a 10x12 space. The new storage company didn't know I had a history of late payments. The first month was free. I was grateful for a fresh start. Gratitude was my strong suit. It served me well.

Every day I worked on the little things. Those things most people learn in their formative years. I missed all that social and emotional growth. It was stunted by alcoholism. I was a teenager in a grown man's body. With a grown man's life.

I moved my belongings, from the old storage to the new one, between what wash jobs. Most of the stuff, was just that – stuff I had obtained over the years of marriage. I was the king of stuff, back then. I had yet to realize that life was not about *stuff*. But rather our relationship with our Creator, and our relationships with our fellow man. By time I got rid of the stuff that didn't matter, the new storage unit was big enough to park my wash trailer, and house a temporary office.

I stacked and stored things neatly, and put down a 6x6 carpet with a desk for my office. A friend of mine tapped into the storages power supply so I could hook up a desk light and my old computer. It was like having my own shop again. It did feel weird telling Teato what to do, as he helped me arrange my little storage compartment shop. For one, because it was a storage compartment. But mostly because I hadn't been fit to be in charge in a long time.

Usually around noon I would say:
"Let's get some lunch."
The look on Teato's face was priceless. There wasn't a single alcohol break, like before, in the entire day. And my cheeks would actually be sore from smiling so much. Life was definitely looking up.

I had a water machine that turned tap water into spot free water. It came with a 1000 gallon holding tank. I took it apart, while I was drunk, and was never able to put it back together – until I got sober. I'd tried to sell it, but taken apart, no one could tell what it was. I was glad that I still had It. It was an important part of the wash business.

I had a friend, Todd, who owned a mobile home park. He let me hook up the machine to his water supply, and keep it behind a short wall that ran in front of his mobile home park. So I always had access to it. He never charged me a cent. And within a couple of days, I had it up in running. But Todd did have his boundaries.
"You're good for now, Chad. But as soon as you get on your feet, this thing will have to go."
Again, I was grateful.
"Yeah, for sure, Todd. Thanks for the hookup."

I went to meetings two and three times a day, called my sponsor daily, and read that Big Book. The other sober members of AA offered to help me out in any way they could. My life got better with every day of sobriety.

Things in life definitely started looking up day by day. I noticed that a simple twenty dollar bill would remain in my pocket for days. When I was drinking it would only last hours. I put 40 dollars of gas at a time in my truck.

I washed my work truck weekly and detailed it monthly. It became my pride and joy. I never realized, before, what a neat freak I was. I didn't care when I was drinking. But when I got sober there was never any clutter or trash in my truck.

That Chevy 1500 truck was a gas hog, and I eventually I decided I needed something more fuel efficient – or rather, my sponsor pointed it out. So I sold the gas guzzler and bought an older utility truck. It had a small bed to the hold water tank, and sliding doors to load my supplies. The owner let me make payments. It seemed the whole universe was now working in my favor.

My priorities were starting to shift. Rather than trying to sport some fancy personal vehicle, I got something I could easily afford – a little 4-cylinder Honda Civic with 225,000 miles on it.

God – the CEO of the universe had thrown me a lifeline. I was in constant contact with my AA sponsor, and working the steps, precisely as he prescribed them. It was like taking medicine. I was getting well. I was becoming whole. Business was picking up too, because I was working for a change. I had to drop one of my daily meetings just to keep up with the demand.

As I approached my 4th month of sobriety, I noticed that I starting to get flooded with feelings of guilt and shame. I'd been a dreadful human being, and my soul was paying the price. Donnie told that it was normal.

"It happens to everyone, Chad. It's part of the recovery process."

"But, Donnie, it's killing me. Why does it bother me so much?"

"Because you've grown a conscience," he explained. "The fourth and fifth steps will relieve the pain. You'll document and confess your defects of character. Then you'll be truly free."

"Donnie, I've done a lot of bad stuff. I don't know if I can..."

"Chad," he interrupted. "We've all done bad things. We're only as sick as our secrets."

That night, after a the meeting, I drove home in my little Honda. I was playing a song called "Sorry" by a band Called Buck-Cherry. I think I cried the whole drive home. But it was a happy cry, now that I look back on it. But it certainly didn't seem like that to me at the time. I pulled over, before I got home, and put eyedrops in my red eyes and straightened up so my parents wouldn't know I'd been crying. After all I was a grown man. I thought I was supposed to be.

At the five month mark I finished my fourth and fifth steps. The catharsis was so complete, that I threw up when it was over. My distorted facial features softened. My eyes were blue again. But most importantly, I was comfortable in my own skin, without drinking.

My father took the golden handshake when he'd left his job. He'd retired early with full benefits. He drove my mother to Los Angeles every week to see a liver specialist. She had to have her stomach drained of the fluids that her liver could no longer process. On a brighter note, my mother quit drinking. Thank God for that. I thought she'd be fine.

I was killing time by putting together a model motorcycle my sponsor bought for me, when my phone rang.
"Hello-hello? is this Chad?"
"Yes, this is Chad."
It was my aunt on my dad's side of family.
"I'm afraid I've got some bad news about your mother."
"Mom? What about Mom?"
"She's in the hospital again. It doesn't look good, Chad."
"What? I just saw her last night. How bad is it?"
"You better get to the hospital."
I was speechless. I tried to swallow as a tear ran down my cheek.
"Chad, are still there?"
"Text me the address, Auntie. I'm on the way."

My emotions careened out of control. I looked up to God.
"Why? Why her? I'm the one you should take – not her."
Mom worshipped religiously. She prayed and went to church. I never even cared about church. Why would God take her. I got on my knees and prayed to God – the One I never cared about.

When I got to the hospital, Mom was gaunt and feeble, with a large stomach and black sunken eyes. All I could think to say was:
"You can't leave yet, Mom. God's not done with me."

Mom was released two days later, with a long road of recovery ahead. After almost losing her, I poured myself even deeper into the steps of AA. Seeing myself as I really was, instead of who I *thought* I was, was truly humbling. I'd been materialistic, self-centered, and egotistical. I knew I had to change, but without God, change is impossible.

Alcohol ruled my life while I was drinking. I hadn't been physically capable of having a romantic relationship with a woman. At about seven months sober, that imperious urge returned, and I sought the company of a woman. My fancy sat upon a woman with seven years sober. She was reluctant at first, because I was still a newcomer. I guess I overwhelmed her with my brutish charm and surfer-boy good looks.

My sponsor warned me not to get into a relationship before I had a year sober.
"You don't even know who you are yet."
I smart-mouth him back.
"At least I know who I don't want to be anymore. I've grown. It'll be fine. You'll see."
The woman I fancied told me that her sponsor warned her too.
"Are you crazy, girl. Chad is a newcomer. He doesn't even know who he is yet."
What the hell was that supposed to mean anyway. I found out later they were right. I didn't know anything about living sober. I wasn't fit to have a goldfish, let alone a girlfriend.

We gave it a shot anyway. She had her life together. She was working the AA program. And she was stable. She had a good job, and two kids. And – lest I fail to mention, she was gorgeous. We tried to be mister and misses AA. We went to meetings together, where she told me how to behave.
"Fake it until you make it," she told me.

I learned how to parrot all the AA lingo, and appear like I had my life together too. She took me to upscale restaurants, where she taught me dining etiquette.
"Start with the silverware on the outside, and work your way in. And turn your wineglass upside down because we're not drinking."
Oh, and she taught me to whip out my bankcard and pay the tab before anyone else at the table. Man, I was just glad I made it through dinner without spilling anything.

She even made appearances at my parents' house – for appearances sake. But in the end we went our separate ways. There just wasn't the spark we'd both hoped there would be. And I went back to accumulating *things*, to fill that God-sized hole in my gut.

It hadn't been the easiest ride – but a fun one, and I finally hit my one year sober mark. I felt so much better about life and all it had to offer. I proudly stood up at the Monday night meeting and took my one year sobriety chip. The experience was exhilarating.

Life was in session. I'd learned to live in the *now*. No longer was I sinking in the quagmire of guilt and shame. No longer was I agitated about things beyond my control. My life was unfolding under the care of a power greater than myself. I came to know Him as Jesus of Nazareth.

Two days later I was at my storage yard. A man named Jason, who I'd met through a mutual friend, called me about washing his mobile tire repair trucks. Business was looking up.

I explained my temporary situation at the storage lot.
"You know, Chad, I'm in the process of leasing a two acre lot with a small house on it. I'm thinking I'll turn the house into office space and use the lot to park my trucks.
I thought he was just asking for my opinion on the matter.
"Sounds like a solid plan to me, Jason."
I wasn't thinking of myself, for a change. I was thinking about what would be best for *him.* But he went on.
"Do you want to sub-lease a small part of lot from me, and a desk in the office area."
"That would be awesome. How much?"
"If you'll wash my trucks for free, you don't have to pay anything."
"Ok, Jason. It's a deal."

Again, I was grateful. I was going to actually have a spot with an address. I'd have an office again. I moved my equipment and supplies over from storage. I even got my water machine, and 1000 gallon holding tank, from the mobile home park and hooked it up at the new lot. God is good. Especially when I move my ego out of His way.

I couldn't have been happier with my life, and this was after only a year of sobriety. I had my own desk, WIFI, and a 20 foot storage bin outside to hold my detailing supplies. I had a *working* spot-free water machine, a dodge utility truck, and my little Honda civic to commute to my parents' house every day.

My mother was feeling better these days and her stomach reduced in size. My parents decided that it would be a good time to visit my little sister, Kim, and her family in Idaho. While they were gone I went to work every day and attended my AA meetings. All this, without any adult supervision.

While my parents were visiting my sister in Idaho, another AA sister caught my eye. This one had been sober just six months longer than me. After hanging out for a few days, we started to date. So much for living without adult supervision.

The woman, and her son lived right across the street from the gym, where I went almost daily to use the treadmill for therapy. I introduced her when my parents got home from their trip. Everyone was cordial, but I heard my father whisper under his breath.
"Here we go again."

It turned out that the trip was good for my mother. She was feeling so much better that they started planning another vacation. After a few months home they were off again. On the way out the door, my father whispered in my ear.
"Don't take chances with your romances."
What the heck was that supposed to mean?

My new girlfriend realized that we really didn't have the same interests in life and dumped me. I remembered what Dad said. So instead of getting into another dead-end relationship, I bought a BMW.

The next morning I woke up and jumped out of bed, took a shower and rushed downstairs. I couldn't wait to drive my new toy to Corona and detail it out. I remember staring at my new car, in my parents driveway. *It's a nice car. But I'll never find happiness in a car. There is no joy without God.* But I still spent three hours waxing it.

When my parents arrived back home from their trip, my

mom was surprised to see a BMW in place of the Honda. But my dad asked:

"What's up with *that*, Chad?"

"My new girlfriend dumped me."

His answered surprised me.

"In that case, good choice."

I was going to do whatever I had to do, to stay on this new track. No more going to bars to hang out drinking Cokes. Nobody wanted me there anyway. I was going to continue to get up early and go to work *every* day. *And,* most importantly I would never stop going to my AA meetings.

I still popped in the bar now and then to ask if anyone wanted their car washed. Even the people at the bars started to realize I was serious about sobriety. I knew because they all quit asking me about it, and so did my friends and family.

An industrial space showed up on my radar. 800 square feet of warehouse space, with 200 square feet of office space was mine to lease, for the asking. And I could ask because I wasn't spending close to 200 dollars a day on liquor and cigarettes. The economy was down and the unit would lease for just 600 hundred a month.

The next business day I called the property manager and told her I was interested. I had a week to scrape up the first and last month's rent. Piece-a-cake. All I had to do was work and not drink up the profit. The basic tenant of sobriety is: don't drink, one day at a time. I drove by the building every day, and watched as they painted and prepped it for lease.

I had the check made out in just three work days. I got the key then drove to the building and went inside. I envisioned what it would look like after I moved in. I had earned the right to envision, as long as my visions were in line with God's will. The next day I showered and went to my morning AA meeting, then drove to Corona to start my move.

Teato and I moved equipment, and what office furniture I had, all day. Teato actually became more cheerful himself, now that I wasn't flushing his future down the toilet with mine. My sobriety became a gift to everyone around me. I would pay my plumber friend to hook up the water machine, rather than asking for a favor.

I drove to the new shop even on Sunday, after church, just to sit at my desk and look at the second chance God had given me. Even the gratitude I felt was a gift from God. Without Him, I was just a flailing, failing drunk. The thought that my parents had never given up on me sent a rush of gratitude through me.

After about three years of sobriety, I found that my worse day sober, was better than my best day drunk. Life was not just better than it was before – it was easier. Fear of failure and economic insecurity was gone. I intuitively knew how to handle situations that used to baffle me. Serenity and peace had replaced worry and self-centeredness. God was doing for me, what I could not do for myself.

CHAPTER 19: WILD RIDE

I've heard it said that nothing worth having comes easy. But God is not a thing, and He *does* come easy, to those that seek Him. And His blessings come easy. That's how you know they're from Him. God's blessings overtake you.

I came home from work one evening and overheard my parents talking about their house in Corona. The one I grew up in. My parents rented it out for years, to cover the mortgage. But now, the mortgage was paid off. But the current longtime tenant put in his notice and was moving out at the end of the month.

"The place is gonna need fixing up before we can rent it out again," Mom was saying.

"A whole lot," Dad added.

They didn't know I was listening. But I thought maybe I could help them.

"Hey, folks. How bout I go over there for a few weeks and fix it up – you know, get it ready for you. Why pay somebody, when I can do it for free?"

Mom looked at Dad, who made a 'sure – why not' gesture. They actually trusted me now. The first question came from my mother, was:

"Where would you sleep?"

I shrugged.

"On the floor in the master bedroom, I guess."

"Let us think it over, Son," my dad offered. "We'll let you know what we decide in a couple days."

They took up my offer the following day.

I'll never forget the day I actually pulled up to the house. They say, "you can never go home again." But here I was actually moving back into the house I had been raised in. Even though it was temporary, it was still emotional. Imagine the memories that would flood your mind, if you got the chance to spend some time in the past. Imagine the wrongs, you could right in your mind. And the healing that could be possible within your soul. For *most* of us, the monsters of childhood become impotent dwarfs, when looked upon as an adult.

God helps those who help themselves. I got an old air mattress to sleep on, and put a mini fridge in the kitchen. I am a firm believer that God works through people. And those that heard about the arrangement kicked in to make sure I was comfortable. People gifted me with all kinds of household necessities: a washer/dryer, a vacuum, and a microwave oven, just to name a few.

I brought my storage totes from the shop. I unpacked them for the first time in years. They contained dishes, silverware, pictures, and all sorts of memorabilia, I'd forgotten I had.

I wasted no time doing the improvements I'd sat out to do. I was so busy doing things at the house that I lost concern for anything beyond those walls. Teato ran the shop in my absence. Before I knew it, I started making that house *my* home, instead of getting it ready for new renter. I convinced my parents that *I* should live there and pay rent. It made perfect sense.

A negotiation was in order. After all, the house was part of my parents retirement plan, and their legacy to their three children. They came up with a rental price they could live with, and we signed a contract to that affect.

Now that I was going to be living there permanently, I went to the DMV and filed a change of address form. It may not be a big deal to *normal* people, but I had a driver's license, car registration and insurance – all with a valid and current address. It was a big deal to *me*.

I changed sponsors, so I could be accountable to someone at the local club. Someone who saw me every day. Even though business was getting better, I now had extra expenses. So I put in plenty of sweat equity to renovate the house. My sober friends helped when an applicable opportunity arose. We repainted the entire interior. Before long the house was completely furnished, with all the amenities a family would need.

My car wash was doing so well that I was able to switch from mobile utility trucks and trailers, to minivans, fabricated to hold all the equipment previously pulled on trailers. On the outsides, I stickered them with my company logo and advertising. Everything in life was breaking my way.

I hadn't dated much (lately) but I was on a few dating websites. A dating guru from one of them suggested everyone get two books: "Choose Yourself," by James Altucher, and "The Secrets of the Millionaire Mind," by Harv T. Ekler."

I read "Choose Yourself," first. It was a great read. But when I started reading "The Secrets of the Millionaire Mind," something inside of me clicked. I wanted to know more. I found myself going to bookstores and buying all kinds of 'Self-Help' books. I read them morning and night. I started registering at 'Self-Help' and 'Law of Attraction' websites, by giving them my email address.

I scoured the internet for YouTube videos by Harv Elker. One night I was home making dinner, while watching a Harv Ekler YouTube video. I had YouTube set for auto play. When Harv was over, a different character showed up.

When I turned to look at the computer screen, there was a guy in his late 40's with red hair named Bob Proctor. He was on a stage with large chalkboards, and a boom microphone hanging in front of him. I laughed when I saw him, but I was too busy making dinner to walk over and click to a different video.

As he talked, he drew a stick person on the chalk board. I was interested in what I was hearing, so I grabbed my dinner plate and sat down to watch more. I was not only fascinated by *what* he was saying, but also with the *way* he was saying it. It just made since. He talked about the mind, and the subconscious mind, and how they worked. And at that moment my new focus was on this Bob Proctor fellow. I remember him pointing out the importance of the repetition of ideas.

"We become what we think about."

This particular offering was called "Born Rich." Over the next few months I listened to this man constantly. When I wasn't at a meeting or at work, I could be found reading or listening to 'Law of Attraction' literature. The information Bob Proctor shared, made all the other material I'd been reading and listening to make since. Bob Proctor promised to teach me how to better my life.

"Clean up your credit so you have some leverage and breathing room," Bob directed.

Shortly after that, I got my company incorporated so that I could build business credit, along with my personal credit. I did all these things by reading and listening to people that understood the Law of Attraction. If we worry about debt, we *stay* in debt. If we build credit, and use it properly, we don't have to worry about debt. When we tell ourselves we are worthy, we attract opportunities.

The 'Born Rich' seminar recommended keeping something called a 'goal card.' It was a small, laminated card made by Proctor's office. One's goals and completion dates were written on the card. And the card was to be kept on their person at all times. I made mine from a 3-by-5 index card I purchased at Walmart.

The coming months were incredible. I was checking goals off my goal card, and adding new ones. My car wash business and bank account sky-rocketed. I put a new Lexus on my goal card, and a new Lexus materialized in my driveway. I saw my house newly stucco'd, weeks before the crew arrived to do the work. I saw my backyard upgraded with a retaining wall and a pool. And poof – there they were. We *are* what we think. And I was thinking success.

Bob's office sent emails about various programs. But I never *saw* myself spending money on seminars, so I never had money for them. But I still saturated my mind with Self-Help material. I ordered 'Positive Thinking' cd's and played them in my wash vans while I worked.

A year later my parents decided to buy another house, and rent theirs out. The house they chose needed remodeling before they moved in. I offered to let them stay at my house (which was technically theirs).

It was pleasant to have Mom and Dad close again. The home cooked meals that Mom made were nice too. What good is success not shared. Dad read the Bible, Mom watched 'The Cooking Channel,' and I sat listening through headphones while watching Bob Proctor videos.

I got an email saying that Bob Proctor was going to be in Los Angeles for a three-day seminar. General admission was 497 dollars. I considered this a rare opportunity to see the man I'd been following for years. And the price was in the hundreds, rather than thousands.

My aunt and uncle would be out of town the weekend of the seminar, so they agreed to let me stay their home in L.A. Perfect timing. My younger cousin would be there to keep me company.

I spent all my free time studying and learning more about Bob Proctor. I wanted to be prepared. I augmented my wardrobe, which consisted of shorts and tank tops, to meet the business-casual dress code. I still had dress shoes from my former married life.

The big weekend was at hand. I parked my Lexus in the underground parking garage at the Los Angeles Airport Hilton. Didn't I feel special? I left my suitcase in the car because I was going to my cousin's house after the first night was over.

When I went in to register, they gave me a travel bag with the logo of the 'Proctor and Gallagher Institute.' It was filled with goodies and gifts, and a workbook for the seminar. The name badge they hung around my neck read:

"Chad from U.S."

I waited anxiously in the lobby, along with hundreds of people from around the world. They opened the ballroom doors, revealing an extravagant affair with dozens of round tables that seated eight guests each. Those, had beautiful red table clothes draped over them. The first two rows were reserved for VIP's. Those tables had black table clothes. The music was loud and up-beat. Laughter and energy abounded, as guests flowed in to take the seats of their choice.

First up was a woman named Gina, who summarized the seminar, and laid out the itinerary for the event. After a lengthy edification she introduced Bob Proctor.

"Would everyone in the room to please stand up and give a warm welcome to Bob Proctor."

The audience gave a raucous applause. I smiled from ear to ear, from the pure excitement of being in the room. The first four hours went by quickly as he talked about our minds and thoughts.

"This weekend is going to change your life." Bob told us.

At one point he introduced his partner in the company.

"Before we go too far, let me introduce my business partner, Sandy Gallagher."

As she spoke, I was shocked to learn that I'd been watching seminars that were recorded in the 80's. I was woefully behind the times.

When the first night was over, everyone schmoozed and rubbed elbows, while they trickled out to take the elevators up to their rooms. I went straight to my car and left for my cousin's house. I was so jazzed that I forgot to get my parking ticket validated, so when I pulled up to the closed gate, I had to pay for a day's parking. I didn't care. I was tired and couldn't wait to get some sleep. I entered my cousin's address in my car's GPS, and drove off.

There was a broken watermain nearby, and the street lights were turned off. My GPS had me going in circles, in the dark. After a frustrating two hours of "Rerouting," I was back in front of the hotel. Disgusted, with an overflowing bladder, I pulled back into the underground parking garage. After taking another parking ticket from the machine, I decided to just pay for a room for the night. I'd flash my AAA card and flop in a king-sized bed on an upper floor. I left my suitcase in the car and took the elevator up to the front desk. it was already 12:40 am and all I wanted to do was sleep.

"I'm sorry, we're all booked."

"You've got to be kidding! Please check for anything at all," I begged.

"We have nothing left in our system, sir. I'm sorry."

At this point sleeping in my car was looking like an option. The seminar would start in just seven short hours. Where would I shower. *Oh yeah – full bladder.* After I used the restroom I took the elevator back down to my car. I intended to call my cousin to ask for directions around the watermain break.

Wouldn't you know it – not a single bar of reception on my cellphone. I was dead tired, on a lower level lot. I didn't relish walking out to get cell service. I gave a dissident yell and drove out, only to pay another parking fee. *The room was only 165 dollars a night, and I've already spent 60 on parking, and 20 on gas driving around for two hours.* And it was only day one.

I called my cousin and he guided me to his house – staying on the phone till I arrived. When I got there he wanted to talk, and I wanted to sleep. After all, it was 2:45 am. And I had to be up by 6 am. But we talked a while. Needless to say, I didn't get much sleep.

The second day didn't started out well, because I was so tired. But at the lunch I booked a room for the second night. The next two days were like Niagara Falls – through a squirt gun: powerful, riveting, genuine and potent. I learned that all the creative power of the universe was at my disposal. If – and only if, I changed my way of thinking

Success favors the bold. Those that dare to do what others are unwilling to do. If we would only declutter our minds of trivia, we stand a chance of hearing the truth. The truth is that believing comes before seeing, and not the other way around. The answers come to those that pose the questions. *And* to those that believe in a future that has yet to be – our own future, as observed through the lens of a new paradigm.

Bob explained that our former paradigms of failure were

nothing short of a multitude of bad habits that we acquired over many years. Our lives can be changed by understanding that we *are* indeed whatever we tell ourselves we are. And the universe will give us whatever we ask for – that is, whatever we think about the most.

Our subconscious mind is the engine of success. It perceives every thought as truth. If you dwell on failure and lack, that's exactly what your subconscious mind will draw to you. Our subconscious can be reprogrammed by positive affirmations and ideas. It believes whatever we turn over to it, and it has no ability to choose between real or false.

I processed those new paradigms over the next few months. Intertwining them with the principles of AA, to become a better person. One of Bob Proctor's associates, a man named Arash, phoned me about a coaching program.
"I will absolutely optimize your trajectory toward success."
I believed what he was telling me. But it sounded expensive.
"So, what do you think, Chad?"
"How much does it cost?"
"It's only 7,000 dollars. And we have an installment plan."
My answer was sincere.
"If I could I would,"
The truth was that if I saw myself doing it, my subconscious would find a way.
"Your negative paradigms won't *allow* you to do it, Chad," Arash told me. "Just remember I'm always here."

There wasn't a day that went by that I didn't think about that phone call. Especially the part about my negative paradigms fighting against me. My negative thoughts had programmed my subconscious to push the opportunity away from me.
"No don't do it, Chad. You can't afford it and *I* won't help you."

God only knew how badly I wanted to participate in the program. But my negative self, told me to forget it.
What are you thinking? You don't even have a credit card.
"Shut up!" I said aloud. "I'm going for it."

I'd put over 10,000 dollars into a Roth IRA. Funny, it didn't even cross my mind until I affirmed that I was going to do it.

Not that I *wanted* to do it – but that I *would* do it.

I called my financial representative and told him my intentions"
"You're crazy! "What are you thinking!"

Bob Proctor warned us.
"Now you're going to find something to commit to. Something fantastic. And those 'negative Nancy's and 'doubting Thomas' are going to try and talk you out of it. They're going to do that because they failed at everything they tried. They failed because they lacked the resolved to stick with it. Most of the time, they didn't even start. Well don't you listen to them. Not for one minute. In fact, stay away from them. Get as far away from them as you can."

There would be a penalty for withdrawing funds early. But there would be a bigger penalty for missing out on this opportunity. The next day I phoned Arash, and told him my plan.
"You won't regret it," he replied.
"I hope not," I said as I rolled my eyes.
"Well *I'm sure* you'll be successful," he shot back "That's the way to look at it."

I closed my IRA account and paid a 400 dollar penalty. I put the money in a savings account and made three, 2,500 dollar payments, to PGI (Proctor Gallagher Institute). I was absolutely determined to get what others had obtained. I was looking forward to it.

One of the videos I watched in the coaching program put it like this:
"As you practice and study the new way of thinking paradigm, your so-called friends and acquaintances will slowly stop hanging around you. You'll be thinking differently than the masses. As your thinking changes, so will your income."

Over the next 12 months that exactly what happened. I was in my third month of coaching, and another seminar was scheduled. I called Arash as soon as it was announced. I thought that since I was being coached by Bob that my seminars would be included. Come to find out I was wrong. So I bought a ticket and I booked my room at the hotel in advance this time.

As time passed, I started to notice more and more of the people I once associated with, stopped calling me as much. And to be fair I didn't really reach out to them either. My life revolved around work, AA, and PGI.

Every Sunday I would go pick up my parents for church. And afterwards we would always go to lunch. I learned that tithing to the church was personally rewarding. We do reap what we sow. If we sow nothing, we reap nothing. Our ships can't come in, if we don't send any ships out. The universe is in motion. It gives to us, if we give. It takes from us, if we take. It's more than a way with words. It's even more than a way of thinking. It is – it must be...a way of life.

Bob talked about good ideas and how, through the use of repetition, they will start to manifest. Repetition in thought, in word, and in action. I set my thoughts on becoming a part of Bob's team. I called Arash and put those thoughts into words. I asked if I could volunteer at the next event. He told me to email Gina (Bob's assistant) because she was in charge of that. So I did.

I received and email from Proctor's office saying they would love it if I could be a volunteer at the next event. I replied.
'I would love it too. I just need a week or so to round up the funds for my ticket.'
Bob's office responded as follows:
'You will receive a free VIP ticket for volunteering. No need to purchase a ticket.'
Wow. *Not only do I get to help out, but I get a free ticket. A VIP ticket to the tables with the black table clothes. This thing really works.*

I wanted to do my best as a volunteer, to show the PGI team that I was a valuable asset. That's how I began to think about myself. And that's exactly what I did. I became known to the staff as a person of value. I've been asked to volunteer at every event since. And I do it with pleasure. I learned to speak of success in the present tense. In doing so, I invite success into the here-and-now.

By the end of my coaching I was almost down to zero of my

former friends. My new friends think, and speak in the parlance of positivity, wealth, and big ideas. There are no bounds to the possibilities, because we believe that opportunity is limitless. And I was ok with that. I spent a lot of time alone, studying the material and really getting to know myself. And I realizing that I don't have to have people always around.

Over the next four or five months my car wash quadrupled in revenue, and I was living a life that I never thought possible. But I found myself saying:

"There's more than this out there."

CHAPTER 20: BOB PROCTOR

My life has definitely taken a change in direction over the last few years. I still attend my AA meetings, but I spend a lot more time reading and studying the works of Bob Proctor. My daily routine has changed. My life no longer revolves around the drink. In the morning I get up and have some coffee while I read before I go to work.

The new building I lease is much larger than my last one, and only a mile from my house. I take pride in having my company growing again. After work, I go home and do some more studying, and watching personal development videos.

Those friends, I am still in contact with, occasionally ask me to go out at night. And I always say I'm busy. But I *really* just want to enjoy the alone-time for study. The results in my life are proof, to me, that these new paradigms work, and all I want to do is learn more. I love to do projects around the house, but I've reached the point of diminishing returns. The house is at peak value for the neighborhood because of all the upgrades.

As final acts of love, I demolished the kitchen and built a beautiful open concept modern kitchen. I installed new carpet, new front doors, and had the whole house re-plastered. I installed wood floors in the kitchen. I had the bathroom redone. I even scraped all the acoustic treatment from the ceiling and re-textured it. Most of the work, I did myself.

I feel I am blessed for sure, but there is more growth to be had. God is not done with me. I continue to go to seminars and study. My social life is in decline because the road to self-improvement is the road less traveled. Trivialities no longer capture my thoughts. When I try to express this new way of thinking to the uninitiated, I just get blank stares – about the same results I got by talking about sobriety at the bar.

Since the upgrades on the house were complete. I decided I was going to go talk to my parents about selling the house. It was a super bowl Sunday weekend when I went to my parents to share my idea.
"Mom and Dad, I think we should sell the house."
"What – are you crazy, Chad?" my mother exclaimed.
Then my dad chimed in from the couch.
"You just put over 100,000 into it. *And* all that time."
"I know, I know. But I want a newer house and I'll take on the monetary shortfall myself."

It took a couple weeks to convince my dad to sell. Convincing Mom was harder. That house had been my mom's and dad's for 45 years. It was part of their retirement. And they owned it free and clear. I'd started looking at other homes before my parents were completely on board.

I found a property that we really liked, and we agreed to sell. There was a realtor in my Tuesday networking group. She met with my parents and listed the house. We accepted an offer that put us into escrow.

Meanwhile, as I was further adjusting my priorities, a customer wanted to buy me out of the lease on my new Lexus. Bob Proctor says we must constantly be mindful of our evolving priorities. Since I wasn't driving it much, I accepted his offer and ordered a brand new truck. A truck has a payload bed. You can't do much hauling in a luxury car.

Not long after we were in escrow, we got a pre-approved

loan. My parents found a *new* listing that grabbed their attention. My phone rang. My mother was so excited, she could barely get the words out of her mouth.

"Chad where are you? I think you're really going to like this one."

"I'm 45 minutes away. I can't leave right now. Is it really that nice?"

From our experience, the pictures always made a house look more desirable than it actually was.

"Well then what time can you get here?"

"Give me two hours and I'll meet you guys at my shop."

But as I reviewed the pictures on my phone, my anticipation grew. I finally arrived at my shop. My parents were both there, raring to go. I followed them to the house. It wasn't going to be shown again until the weekend, but the owner was home, and let us in, so that I could see it for myself.

The pictures didn't come close to doing it justice. It was a 2007, 2700 square feet single story home with hardwood floors throughout, and high ceilings with crown moldings. There were three large bedrooms and an even larger master bedroom. It had two full bathrooms and a half-bath in the hall. The backyard sported a beautiful pool/spa. The house had an attached three car garage, and was topped with a brand new solar power system on the roof. The asking price was way too low. The owner expected a bidding war that coming weekend.

We offered 10,000 dollars over the asking price, with a stipulation for an answer by midnight the next day, or we would walk. I didn't think anything about it because I thought that was never going to happen. The house was too good to be true. As soon as that negative thought came bubbling up, I replaced it with a mental picture of me living there.

So I wasn't surprised when we got an email from his realtor stating that they accepted the offer. We closed after a 30 day escrow with a two week rent back. I got the keys while my parents were out of town. I was like a kid at Christmas, up all night making trips with just my new truck that only held so much per load. After two weeks of moving and painting I was finally settled in our new investment home.

When my mind cleared of moving, a new goal formed in my mind. *I can't wash cars forever*. The thought of getting up at 5 am and washing cars when I got old wasn't very attractive. What I wanted to do was teach this information that Bob Proctor was teaching, and help others achieve success in their life. Bob says it thusly:

"You'll never acquire true wealth, without making other people wealthy in the process."

So I inquired into becoming a consultant with Bob Proctor's team, PGI. They have a program that helps you set up your own business as a consultant. It was kind'a pricey, but you get what you pay for. Money has to be in motion to have real power.

Something inside was pulling me toward the consultant coaching program. Or rather pulling *it* toward *me*. And I looked back at all the monumental blessings that overtook me since I started following Bob Proctor. Those were the proofs, and they provided the motivation to join the team. I put a big chunk of money down and then made payments for five months until it was paid for. I had no idea that the training consisted of week-long sessions, that weren't even included in program – three times a year, in Toronto Canada.

After completing three sessions, I am a full time Personal Development Coach. But I still have my car wash to run. At my last training session, as I was in my hotel room, I made a decision to sell my car wash. When I got back to the United states I met with a business broker. We gathered all the business paperwork and listed the business for sale.

I'm looking positively forward to the next chapter of my life. But most importantly I want to convey to you that God works in mysterious ways. You never know what God has in store for you. Not until you can imagine receiving it.

CHAPTER 21: POSITIVE THINKING

After years of study, I have come to develop a clear understanding of the laws of the universe. The first thing I had to do was set aside any conception or belief I previously held on God, the universe, and how to live life.

One of the things I have come to understand is that we think in pictures. If you're wondering what I mean by that just check it out. Go ahead and think of your house, your car, your refrigerator – or anything for that matter. An image of the thing you're thinking about will instantly appear on the screen of your mind.

This baffled me! But I accepted the idea only to find out there is so much more to learn. The instant image was just one part of the psychic construct. When asked to fetch an image of my mind, I couldn't produce one. You try it. I'll wait.

Some of you might have gotten an image of your brain. But your brain is not your mind at all. The is just a switching station for your mind. So without an image of our mind we have confusion, instead of order, because our mind wants an image.

It wants an image, to eliminate confusion.

So, because we think in pictures, our mind gets confused when there is no picture to ponder upon. The only way to get order in our mind is through pictorial visualization, or by looking at the real object. Our mind can be divided into two parts; the conscious mind and the subconscious mind. The conscious mind – our thinking mind, is what we use to contemplate, communicate and make choices.

But the subconscious mind carriers out the subordinate actions required to act on the choice. When we consciously decide to take a shower, we don't need to think about the subroutines involved in the taking of the shower. Our subconscious mind takes the shower while our conscious mind decides what we'll do next.

We go through the cycle dozens of times a day, without even realizing it. Our conscious mind uses the five senses to determine our day-to-day thinking, based upon our outside circumstances to build an image, before impressing that image onto our subconscious mind.

Now on the other hand, we have the subconscious mind which is in control of the tasks our body performs on a daily basis. The subconscious mind, unlike our conscious mind, has no ability to think or make decisions. In fact, it must obey exactly what the conscious mind tells it to do. It must follow the program (paradigm).

We, as humans, take in what our outside circumstance is showing us, through our sensory factors, and impresses it onto our subconscious mind. And in return, our subconscious produces results, in exact harmony with what the conscious mind impressed upon it.

We become what we think about. The notion of changing the picture on the inside, without the use of our perceived circumstances as a model, hit me like a ton of bricks. We can change our reality, independent of our circumstance. The first step in the process can be summed up in one word – repetition.

The idea that we have to impress the image of what we want, over and over again, onto our subconscious was absurd to me at first. And when I was told to start doing a lot of reading, and to read the same thing over and over again, I burst into laughter. That was insane! But my mentor said I would have the same results as him. So I did it.

We attract what we focus on the most. This law of attraction thing really got a hold of me. As I learned more about the conscious and the subconscious minds, I was introduced to our 'intellectual factors:' memory, intuition, reason, perception, and will. They operate with, and though, our body and soul to allow us to become anything we want.

These human-ranked intellectual factors cannot be found in animals. They have their own grade of sensory factors and don't come with intellectual factors the way humans do. Animals can only grow up to be whatever they born to be at birth. The same goes with a carrot seed, or an apricot seed. They have no ability to change what they are. But we as humans can. And that's exactly what I was taught to do. And it was easy.

If you hold the image of what you want in your mind, and repeat that image over and over again until it is imprinted on the subconscious, it will eventually take form in the real world. There are ways to accomplish this. Let's take a look at some of them.

<u>Acting as if</u>

If our subconscious mind is a dumb terminal and does whatever the conscious mind impresses on it, then wouldn't it be a good idea to act as if the desired outcome has already been manifested? One might ask:
"How can I act as if I am wealthy when I'm broke?"

Your subconscious mind doesn't know you're broke, or what you look like, or what you drive. It doesn't know what's in your bank account. It only knows what you impress upon it. So act like the person you want to be, and the subconscious mind will produce whatever is given to it.

Changing Paradigms

There is something else that blocks the things we want in our lives. Paradigms: a group of habits and beliefs that have been programed in our psyche over a period of time. We can act *as if* all day long, but until we change our paradigms there will be little change in our lives.

The paradigm is the blocker that keeps the subconscious mind thinking and doing what it was previously programmed to do. And the only way to change that paradigm is by an emotional impact, or rigorous repetition of study. In order to purposely reprogram our subconscious mind, we must bombard it with repetition – over and over again until a new paradigm overrides our old way of thinking.

The Power of the Universe

Another lesson to understand is the power of the universe, and how we can use this power to impress our new idea/image onto our subconscious mind. We must become emotionally involved with our idea and begin, at once, to manifest it in our reality. This technique is taught by way of meditation.

Meditation

If we quiet the mind for 15 or 20 minutes at a time, and maybe put on some soothing music, we can relax and clear the mind. Eliminate all distractions, like your phone, or outside noise, or TV. Then free your mind of any care in the world.

You can even go so far as to feel as if your body weighs 500 pounds, and that you can't even lift your arms or legs. Then start to visualize what you want in life. Maybe how much you would like to give to your church or favorite charity. Or the house you want to live in, or the vacations you want to take. And really see yourself doing or living these images.

While you're in that relaxed state, the images you hold on the screen of your mind, have a better chance of transferring into your subconscious mind. Free of distraction, lighten your body and imagine how good it will feel to have accomplished these things. Remember, if you go there in the mind, you can go there in the body.

A lot of people I come across today tell me that they are already calm and collected. But their actions say otherwise. Drama and peace cannot abide in one vessel. If someone wants to learn to meditate, and attract new and positive things into their life, they have to learn how to be calm.

My good friend, Dr. Michael Barron wrote the most comprehensive book I've ever read on the art of meditation. It's titled "The Method of Surrendering." You can order it on Amazon.com. It really did help me to be calm, more powerful, and draw closer to our Creator.

Self-Image

Your self-image, and self-talk are keys to changing your reality as well. What we think of ourselves gets directly pipelined to our subconscious mind. It cannot tell if what you're thinking and saying is true or false, good or bad. It just mirrors our thoughts, with absolute fidelity. Feed it with positivity and you will receive positive results in your life. It's that simple.

CHAPTER 22: GIFTS FROM GOD

Today I recognize the gifts and insights given to me by The Father of Lights. Every morning as I wake up, before my feet even hit the floor, I thank God for my life. I pour my coffee, sit down and write a daily Gratitude list. I write 10 things I'm thankful for.

Throughout the day I thank God for the life lessons I learn that day. And when my day is done, as I climb into bed, I say my prayers. I grab a small rock from my night stand – my gratitude rock. And I give thanks for the gift that stood out *most* to me during my day. I go to sleep with a smile on my face – just for being alive and sober.

A lot of my story took place before I became aware of the

power of God. And also, before changing my thinking. I was given gentle, and not so gentle, nudges along my journey through life. But I failed to sense them, until God hit me in the head with that 2-by-4 of alcoholic paralysis. Hopefully, it doesn't take all that for *you* to see the light.

When I was young, God blessed with an entrepreneurial mindset. I sold golf balls, or painted curbs, or made cinnamon toothpicks. Other blessings came when I got sober. Sobriety changed everything. A growing relationship with God changed everything again. I received of all kinds of material gains in my early years. Only to lose them through riotous living.

But through that loss I learned the most valuable lessons. Money isn't everything. And, God doesn't bless us with abundance so we can worship at the altar of materialism. God prospers us, so that we can bless others. The pipe that transfers fresh water, is always rushing with fresh water. A clogged pipe stagnates.

When I started studying Bob Proctor's works, my life changed for the better *again*. I started thinking my way into positive results. The more I am grateful for the blessings that come my way, and the more that I bless others, the more blessings I will surely receive. Blessed are those that sow, for they will always have seed.

I have come to realize that if I'm grateful for things that have meaning: family, health, food and clean water; that the universe will take care of any material gain I might enjoy. As I learned about gratitude and giving, the things that money can't buy, like joy and optimism started to manifest in my life.

I had an ice cold hole in my soul for years. A hole that I tried to fill with *things*. When I asked God into my heart, all that changed. And I found that *He*, having given me His Spirit, would not withhold any other good thing.

As I look back over the past few years, the material gifts God has given me are better, and more lasting, than any material gain I'd tried to finagle for myself. My cup overflows with blessings, too numerous to humbly catalog.

By far, the fastest way to receive anything in life, is through the power of giving. Giving without any expectations for something in return. And if you don't have much to give, you can give what is most precious to the human condition. You can give of your time. Yes, you can give the gift of your time, and you can start immediately. If you don't like what you're receiving, you might want to take a good look at what you're giving out.

CHAPTER 23: THE VIEW FROM MY ENGINE

We live in the *caboose* of life, metaphorically speaking. The view from the caboose is a result of where the engine traveled a hundred train-cars before. We cannot change our future by thinking about the direction the caboose is traveling. Change in direction takes place in the engine, based on the options provided by the train tracks. Through positive thinking and changing our paradigms, we can even change the lay of the tracks.

Here is the view looking through the window of my faith-engine. I see my family living in a large 5,000 square foot ranch style home that overlooks the city. I see two vacation homes; one in Hawaii, and the other in the mountains. I am married to the women of my dreams. A woman who loves life just as I do. I pour good paradigms into our children, and positively impact their lives.

I see us worshiping God faithfully, and praying together as a family. I fancy us driving a brand-new, red Ferrari Spider and a Cadillac Escalade. I have a large office with over 50 consultants working with me, to help teach this powerful information on personal development. Together, we are helping make peoples' dreams come true.

My family is very important to me. I am on a mission to free them from worry, doubt, and debt, so that their lives are full of opportunity and fortune. I work from my office, or my house, or from remote travel all over the world. I travel the world on speaking engagements. We take frequent vacations to rest and recuperate. I travel on my own personal jet, at the moment of opportunity. I have a staff that keeps track of all my appointments and arranges my speaking tours.

I give very large chunks of my revenue to the charities or churches of my choice. I give money to help build schools in Africa for under-privileged children.

This is the first of multiple books that I write. I am a New York Times best-selling author. My books are translated into different languages, so that my teaching reaches, and helps everyone in the world. I keep a large yacht at the harbor, not too far from where we live. We take it out and enjoy the ocean and the sea-breeze while we relax. We invite friends to go out for short cruises and entertainment.

My 'Unlock Wealth' subsidiary has become a huge name in the self-help industry, and is advertised daily by my multimedia experts. I understand that the more people I helped in life, yesterday, the more I will be rewarded today. And helping people is what I do best.

More about Thinking Into Results

As I traveled through my journey of life I became more aware of my own inner-self. As I studied how our mind and body works, it became very clear to me that a large portion of the population is in the need of financial freedom. Most of us spend so much our time earning a living, and worrying about bills, that we have no time (or energy) to express our true desires.

I'm not saying that money should be our primary purpose in life, but it *can* make life more enjoyable, if viewed through the proper lens. Money is a tool. Tools are of no value if they lay idle.

I noticed that a very large number of people don't get what they want, because they don't have the funds available to have it. People often go without meals for lack of money for the most basic of necessities. People would give more if they had more. But most people say to themselves, and others, that they don't have wants or needs. And that they just fine going without. If they got honest with themselves they'd realize that are just making themselves feel better about not having purchasing power.

As I studied Bob Proctor's philosophies, I became aware of things I never knew before. I was raised with different views on a lot of things about life, and about our behavior in general. It wasn't until a couple years after I started to study Bob's philosophies that I came across the paradigm of 'Thinking Into Results.'

Bob pointed out lessons I'd learned through the school of hard knocks. The very first lesson in 'Thinking Into Results' is learning how to set and achieve goals. Many of us stumble our way to unsustainable breakthroughs, but don't really have repeatable and sustainable processes for success.

What Bob does, in this magnificent program, is teach us about the power of REPETITION. It's a word you're going to hear throughout the program. By setting our goals in life, and getting them down on paper, we automatically begin shift our thinking. Then the real fun begins as we go through the 12 lessons and learn all about our minds and our bodies. We will come to realize how we have always achieved things in life, unconsciously.

In the 12 lessons from 'Thinking into Results,' you will find that each lesson builds to the next. You go from; how to set goals in lesson one, to bridging the gap between knowing and doing in lesson two. You will then cease setting goals that you never achieve.

In lesson three you will learn about your infinite mind, and how you can use it to achieve anything you want. You will start to see results before you go on to:

Lesson 4 - The Secret Genie
Lesson 5 - Thinking into Results
Lesson 6 - Environment is but our Looking Glass
Lesson 7 - Trample the Terror Barrier
Lesson 8 - The Power of Praxis
Lesson 9 - The Magic Word
Lesson 10 - The Most Valuable Person
Lesson 11 - Leaving Everyone with the Impression of Increase
Lesson 12 - Magnifying your Mind

I used to think that all I ever wanted in life was available to me, if I sold enough, invested enough, or worked hard enough. After I started this program, I shook my head. I could have gone through life much easier and with more abundance, and more prosperity, if I understood these new concepts in my younger days. I would have bypassed all the chaos.

As I went through the lessons, it was like my inner voice came alive, and started agreeing with all that was being taught. I started to see my life in a totally different way. And as I started to think differently, my life started becoming different. It was like finding the lost lid to a puzzle box. I had all the puzzle pieces without knowing what the puzzle looked like put together.

All the information I had gathered or studied over the previous years came together as I went through 'Thinking Into Results.' My inner self spoke to me and guided me to not only write this book, but to spend the rest of my glorious days on earth helping others to achieve their birthright. We – all of us, are born wealthy. The inborne gifts God gave us at birth are sufficient for us to thrive and prosper. But unopened gifts are but useless decorations.

What happened for me, can happen for you too. Go to

unlockwealth.net and watch the short video introduction from the master teacher himself, Bob Proctor. Then, If you want to change your life, feel free to contact me at unlockwealth.net. And let's have a talk.

Everything in life works by the law of cause and effect. When you understand the universal laws taught in the 'Thinking into Results' system, your whole world will change. And the best part is that the change will be permanent .

The End

ABOUT THE AUTHOR

Self-made millionaire, Chad Reynolds, is a longtime follower of Thinking into Results pioneer, Bob Proctor. Chad, being aware of the potential power of positive thinking, wants to share his new paradigms with as many readers as possible. Chad is a devout Christian. He encourages you to focus on building a relationship with the Creator of the universe – the Primal Source of all insight and creativity. Chad wants help you evolve into a better you – the best you. For only by helping others do we find true wealth.

Made in the USA
San Bernardino, CA
24 January 2019